Praise for *Famous Florida Recipes*

"Open this book to any page and you will find the alchemy and allure of true Florida." —Lisa Young Jensen, Florida Department of Agriculture and Consumer Services

"This book is much more than a cookbook. It offers a glimpse into the rich diversity of Florida's different regions, introducing those regional foodways and explaining how the recipes reflect, the people and their histories." —Lucy M. Long, PhD, Center for Food and Culture, Bowling Green, Ohio

"*Famous Florida Recipes* takes readers for a delicious ride across Florida and its extraordinary past." —Gary R. Mormino, University of South Florida–St. Petersburg

FAMOUS FLORIDA RECIPES

Famous
Florida Recipes

Centuries of Good
Eating in the
Sunshine State

LOWIS CARLTON

ILLUSTRATIONS BY
JOSEPH BROWN, JR.

REVISED BY MARISELLA VEIGA

 Pineapple Press

Palm Beach, Florida

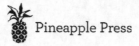

Pineapple Press
An imprint of Globe Pequot, the trade division of
The Rowman & Littlefield Publishing Group, Inc.
4501 Forbes Blvd., Ste. 200
Lanham, MD 20706
www.rowman.com

Distributed by NATIONAL BOOK NETWORK

Library of Congress Cataloging-in-Publication Data available

Names: Carlton, Lowis, author. | Veiga, Marisella, author.
Title: Famous Florida recipes : centuries of good eating in the sunshine
  state / Lowis Carlton ; illustrations by Joseph Brown, Jr. ; revised by
  Marisella Veiga.
Description: 2nd edition. | Lanham, MD : Pineapple Press, [2023] | Includes
  index. | Summary: "This little cookbook is a favorite of many
  Floridians. For more than ten years, Lowis Carlton traveled Florida,
  collecting and testing recipes found to be popular with different
  cultures in all the regions of the state. Iconic recipes include Greek
  lamb kabobs from Tarpon Springs, fried Catfish from Clewiston, beef
  barbecue from Florida cow country, Key West paella, and yam praline pie
  from the Panhandle. Recipes are grouped by region and each section is
  preceded by a mini history"-- Provided by publisher.
Identifiers: LCCN 2022053944 (print) | LCCN 2022053945 (ebook) | ISBN
  9781683343509 (paperback) | ISBN 9781683343516 (epub)
Subjects: LCSH: Cooking--Florida. | LCGFT: Cookbooks.
Classification: LCC TX715 .C268 2023 (print) | LCC TX715 (ebook) | DDC
  641.59794--dc23/eng/20221122
LC record available at https://lccn.loc.gov/2022053944
LC ebook record available at https://lccn.loc.gov/2022053945

Contents

ABOUT THE AUTHOR

Lowis Carlton has written for a variety of national publications and is also the author of the book *Florida Seafood Cookery*. She was graduated magna cum laude from the University of Miami with a BA and MA in English and was named to Phi Kappa Phi. She also holds a BS in Home Economics from Florida International University, where she concentrated on work with the chefs in the school's highly rated hotel school.

While food editor for the *Miami Herald*, Lowis won the Vespa Award, a national newspaper award for food writing. She served as a judge for the Pillsbury Bake-Off and traveled extensively in Europe studying food customs.

Lowis was gourmet editor for *Palm Beach Life* magazine, as well as a columnist for the Florida Department of Agriculture, writing about Florida products for 200 newspapers throughout the United States.

After residing in Miami for many years, Lowis and her then semi-retired husband moved to St. Lucie West, Florida. Lowis continued developing and testing recipes, participating in church functions, and writing Florida fiction. The Carltons enjoyed world travel, bridge, fishing, and the recipes contained in this book and others in her extensive cookbook collection.

Lowis Carlton died in Chattanooga, Tennessee, in 2016.

ABOUT THE REVISER

Marisella Veiga was born in Havana, Cuba, and raised both in Miami, Florida, and St. Paul, Minnesota. Her writing has appeared in numerous national and international literary and commercial publications. Her book *We Carry Our Homes with Us: A Cuban American Memoir* details her family's early years in exile.

She has received the Evelyn La Pierre Award in Journalism, the Canute M. Brodhurst Prize for short fiction as well as a Pushcart Prize Special Mention in Fiction. She was a syndicated columnist with Hispanic Link News Service. She was a featured home cook at the Florida Folklife Festival in White Springs, Florida.

Along with Cuban home cooking demonstrations, Veiga continues researching and writing about food and foodways—Cuban and now

Floridian. Over decades of living and working in Florida, she intentionally set out to learn its history and become familiar with all parts of the state so as to better love it. As a result, Marisella Veiga is at home in rural settlements and urban centers throughout the Old Peninsula.

FOREWORD

The late Lowis Carlton's love for and celebration of Florida is evident. She highlighted portions of regional histories and collected recipes from communities to share the bounty with a wider audience. Much has changed since her last update of her book in 1997. Part of my work in this new edition has been to clarify historical facts, elaborate where needed, and provide new information. Textboxes now highlight important facts. All the recipes from the original edition remain.

In addition, I have been graced with the work of gathering more recipes. Some are missed classics; others are on the way to becoming classics. I added more than sixty new recipes—simple to complex but never daunting.

Home cooks provided the majority of the recipes. Yet some food industry professionals are also contributors. The recipes I collected are noted by a "Courtesy of . . ." beneath the recipe's title. Often, notes about the cooks or recipe origins are included. Contributors' generosity has

Regional Key to Florida Cooking

been the underlying force for this edition. I am grateful for contributors from Pensacola to the Keys—old friends and new ones.

Florida continues to attract people of all ages and from all places. You'll find recipes from newer residents who have brought their traditional foods. Many, many groups' cuisines are not present, as I focused on one or two majority-minority groups from a particular area. To have all today's Florida communities represented calls for an even more comprehensive cookbook.

Over the years, I broadened my palate from my grandmother's Spanish Cuban cooking in our family's Miami kitchen. As a young adult, I drove north from Miami to see Lake Okeechobee for a new cultural experience. Clewiston provided a first real taste of Florida Southern cooking: a plate of fried catfish with hush puppies and coleslaw. Every now and again, I drive a little way for the same meal in the nearby rural communities of Hastings or Crescent City. There's nothing like a meal in the place from which the foods have recently been harvested.

First tastes are generally delightful. Many have joined the repertoire of what I cook and serve at home or bring to potlucks. The foods of my native island still reign, but so many dishes from other communities bless our table. Adopting new foods is one way for people to begin to assimilate, part of the pathway to slowly become Floridians.

Our lively cuisine has resulted from talented, skilled cooks who were often willing or forced to take risks along with a mix of ingredients and methods from many cultural, ethnic, and religious groups: Native American, African, European, and Asian. Where Southern cooking predominates, in the northern and central parts of the state, it is important to note that African Americans made a huge contribution to the cuisine.

It has been a pleasure to gather these recipes and a joy to try many of them in the process. Award-winning ones are found among ones that should win awards.

Enjoy reading and start cooking!

Marisella Veiga
St. Augustine, Florida

Historic
Northeast Florida

Gates of old St. Augustine, the oldest continuously settled U.S. city, founded in 1565.

A picturesque lighthouse stands as a stately sentinel at Amelia Island along the coast of north Florida where the United States really began. Amelia Island is our state's most northern barrier island.

On April 3, 1513, Juan Ponce de León first landed on Ponte Vedra Beach, near the harbor of yet-to-be-named St. Augustine. He was amazed and delighted at the wealth of foliage in this temperate land of sunshine and blue skies. But he set sail, seeking a nonexistent Fountain of Youth.

At that time, the Timucuans, who passed on their wonderful oyster roasts still enjoyed today, lived here. They farmed corn, beans, and other vegetables. They smoked and dried fish, including whale, which they traded with inland natives, according to historian Susan Parker. About 200,000 Timucuans lived in northeast Florida and southeast Georgia at the time of European arrival. Moors and free Africans came with the Spanish Conquistadors and brought their foods including lentils, cumin, okra, eggplant, yam, and sugarcane. Spanish favorites were chickpeas, chorizo, garlic, sherry, rice, and wheat. Pigs, cows, and chickens were the domesticated livestock brought to this hemisphere by the Spanish. Later, in 1565, Spain sent her top-ranked admiral Pedro Menéndez de Avilés to seize the harbor and all land from Labrador to Mexico. Eventually the Spaniards built a string of forts from Cape Florida to Santa Elena, with St. Augustine's coquina rock structure, Castillo de San Marcos, as the headquarters, begun in 1672. The Franciscan missions were established along with the flavors and foods of Spain. Pigs were free-roaming and today's wild boars are their descendants. Later, Low Country Anglo and African settlers and others from New England and Virginia made their way further south into Florida. The Anglos preferred fewer seasonings; their culinary strong points were sweets and quick breads. English tastes joined the mix of what had fused at various levels: native, African, Moorish, and Spanish cooking.

New cultures continued to arrive from the Mediterranean with a band of Minorcans late in the 1700s. These industrious people—among them Greeks and Italians—established new customs and introduced new foods. Dr. Andrew Turnbull brought them as indentured servants to work on his indigo plantation in New Smyrna. Descendants of the original groups still cook their traditional dishes, regularly seen on local menus as well as annual festivals and other community and private gatherings.

It was not until July 10, 1821, that the Stars and Stripes fluttered over the fort, after secession of Florida from Spain. The embattled little community fought through the Seminole Indian Wars—of which there were three—then became a "state of the American nation" in 1845. Throughout the second Seminole War from 1835 to 1842, national newspapers reported such news as how Indians were tricked into capture under a flag of truce, and the escape of Osceola's men from the dungeon in the fort. They told of the Indian leader's seizure and imprisonment while on his way to confer with American leaders seven miles from St. Augustine. His death in Fort Moultrie, South Carolina, caused much bitterness, for public sentiment was with the Seminoles, but things calmed down when the war finally ended.

The town was in Union hands from 1862 to the end of the War Between the States in 1865. There was a long slumberous period until 1874, when the first locomotive arrived and tourists began coming to St. Augustine.

Henry M. Flagler, enchanted with the air of the drowsy, former little Spanish town, started the renaissance of St. Augustine in 1885, with the Hotel Ponce de León. Thus, the town was launched as a winter resort for the very wealthy. Flagler extended a railroad southward and made the city headquarters for the Florida East Coast Railway and Hotel System. The hotel eventually became part of Flagler College and the railroad buildings are now student dormitories.

Flagler asked a cousin, Thomas Horace Hastings, to establish a farm outside St. Augustine for growing vegetables to supply the needs of his hotel guests. In 1890 Hastings and his family founded a settlement on 1569 acres, the Prairie Garden plantation. The surrounding rural community incorporated in 1909 and Hastings calls itself Florida's potato capital. Today, growers in St. Johns, Putnam, and Flagler counties produce the bulk of the potato crop. St. Johns County produced 8,000 acres of combined table stock and chipping potatoes last season.

Nearby Armstrong was an early African-American settlement begun circa 1886 around a sawmill, then the railroad was extended there. Armstrong is the most southern stop of the Gullah Geechee Cultural Heritage Corridor, a National Heritage area. The Gullah Geechee are a cultural group composed of descendants of West African slaves. Skilled rice growers, they were brought to work plantations in the Carolinas, Georgia, and Florida. Most stayed in the Low Country, maintaining a distinctive dialect and strong sense of family and place.

St. Augustine has kept its atmosphere of ages past, with its horse-drawn carriages, the old fort, and coquina rock houses with Spanish balconies. The combination of Spanish, Minorcan, Cuban, African,

Southern, and indigenous foods and foodways are found in contemporary cooking in our nation's Oldest City.

Seasonings were—and still are—spicy, heavy on thyme, tomatoes, and onions, and, at times, a fiery hot, flavorful pepper called Datil, believed brought to North America by the Turnbull colonists.

Pilau was so much in favor in time past that when it couldn't be made with chicken, pork, ham, or shrimp, it was filled with speckled butter beans for a meatless main dish. The dish remains popular, especially at large family meals, church dinners, and annual festivals.

Other early day recipes for clam chowder, boiled mullet, and yellow rice are still made. At Easter, there are traditional recipes once used to make treats given to street singers who serenaded the families—some sweet foods, some hot. Two favorites are Fromajardis, cheese-stuffed baked pastries, and Minorcan crispees, baked pastry circles sprinkled with cinnamon sugar.

South of St. Augustine is the lively city of Daytona Beach, famous for its twenty-three-mile-long beach of pure white, hard-packed sand. Built along the Atlantic on the Halifax River, Daytona began with the establishment of Spanish missions late in the sixteenth century. Many Timucuans converted to Christianity before the English conquered the area in 1763. British plantation owners were succeeded by Spanish during their second period in Florida. Finally, in the nineteenth century, Georgia colonists built sugar plantations and stayed permanently.

The town was named Daytona in 1870 by Mathias Day, and the word "Beach" was added in 1924. While today the city is better known for NASCAR, fewer pines, palmetto, and cabbage palm thrive outside the city. In the spring, orange and grapefruit blossoms from citrus groves used to perfume the air.

Davidson Brother's Citrus has been in Daytona Beach since 1922. It remains a family-run business shipping oranges, tangerines, honeybells, and grapefruit. Their groves are mostly further south in Rockledge and Ft. Pierce.

Follow the St. Johns River—the nation's longest north-flowing river—from its birthplace in Sanford to arrive in Jacksonville, a busy seaport that is one of the state's major cities.

It was near the mouth of the St. Johns River that Jean Ribault and a party of French Huguenot explorers anchored on April 30, 1562, marking the discovery of the river by Europeans. Ribault marked it a French possession. In 1564, 250 French Huguenot colonists followed. At the foot of the hill now called St. Johns Bluff, they planted their colony, calling it Fort Caroline. After Ponce de León claimed all Florida for Spain, Pedro Menéndez de Avilés was sent to wipe out the French settlement, which he did. He returned in triumph to his camp, where he established St. Augustine.

Because it was a good place to ford the river, the Native American Timucuans called Jacksonville Wacca Pilatka, translated into English as Cowford. The English developed the Indian Trail from below St. Augustine north to the Cowford, then to Georgia into the "King's Highway."

In 1816, Lewis Zachariah Hogans became Jacksonville's first settler, and a few frame cabins were built. Late in June 1822, the town was surveyed and named in honor of General Andrew Jackson. At the end of the Second Seminole War in 1842, the city began its climb to its modern status. Today, it is one of Florida's major cultural, financial, medical, industrial, transportation, and commercial centers. The world-renowned Mayo Clinic opened in Jacksonville in 1986. Downtown development includes the Riverwalk, a landscaped, two-mile area that once hosted various businesses restaurants, shops, and marina on the banks of the St. Johns River. Today it is largely green space. The downtown also boasts a Skyway Express people mover and a campus of Florida State College at Jacksonville. The city's food scene is vibrant.

Just one of the numerous bridges spanning rivers and waterways is the award-winning Napoleon B. Broward suspension bridge soaring over the St. Johns River, with towers reaching 472 feet. It is known as the Dames Point Bridge.

This north Florida city retains an old-time Southern charm, with some neighborhoods that have palatial homes. The city maintains lushly landscaped parks and everywhere you look are many varieties of tall oaks draped with Spanish moss, magnolia, hickory and cedar trees, pines, crepe myrtles, and many other examples of flora that thrive in temperate climates.

Home port for a big shrimp fleet is Mayport, a community between Naval Station Mayport and the St. Johns River. It is part of the Jacksonville Beach communities. Mayport shrimp is wild Atlantic-caught and includes those found around northeast Florida: white, pink, brown, and a deep-water cousin called rock shrimp. Though known in northeast Florida, this hard-shelled shrimp is more bountifully harvested in waters off Cocoa Beach. Rock shrimp appeared on the market during the 1980s. Titusville is known for it, especially famous at a local restaurant, Dixie Crossroads.

In reality, our shrimping industry's birthplace in the late 1880s is a little further north in Fernandina, on Amelia Island. Shrimping boats are still working and the town celebrates its heritage with an annual festival. In short, northeast Florida is our shrimp capital.

Along with traditional Southern fare, in particular vegetable side dishes, seafood and fish such as grouper, snapper, and dolphin are popular, especially on backyard barbecue grills as well restaurant menus.

A Great Floridian: Solicito "Mike" Salvador

The Sicilian-born seaman (b. 1869) became a leader in our shrimping industry. He came first to Fernandina Beach, Amelia Island, when a hurricane caused his Italian ship to lay over there. He worked both as an interpreter and fisherman on boats to New Orleans, Cedar Key, and returned to Fernandina by 1889. Shrimping industry innovations include experiments with preserving and canning shrimp, using large shipments to access refrigerated car lots, and haul siene use. He modified otter trawl nets to increase catch and fish deeper waters.

The Mike Salvador, Salvatore Versaggi (a brother-in-law), and Anthony Poli families expanded shrimping to St. Augustine in 1922. By 1925, Versaggi shrimp boat captains and crews caught 200,000 to 300,000 pounds of shrimp annually, according to the St. Augustine Lighthouse and Maritime Museum exhibit "Shrimping Ain't Easy." By the 1960s, the catch grew to 3.5 million pounds. Today, the Versaggi family maintains operations in the Tampa area.

...

Frogmore Stew or Low Country Boil

Courtesy of Dorothy Dornblaser

5 lbs. red bliss potatoes, scrubbed clean (cut in half or quartered if large)
4 lbs. Kielbasa sausage, cut into 3-inch pieces
12 whole ears fresh corn, cleaned and halved
6 lbs. fresh shrimp, heads off (21–25 count)
4 whole lemons, halved
4 medium onions, halved
1 cup Zatarain's or Old Bay Seasoning
3 Tbsp. salt
(Can also include mushrooms, carrots, scallops, etc.)

The best container to use for cooking is a 30 qt. stock pot with basket (for propane burner). When boiling, add Kielbasa. Ten minutes later, add the potatoes. Five minutes later, add the corn/mushrooms, and other vegetables. Ten minutes later, add the shrimp and scallops. Wait three minutes and it's done.

Total time cooking is 28 min.

Serves 12.

Originally from St. Helen's Island, South Carolina, Frogmore Stew went south to north Florida and stayed. A few cooks with varying skill levels can work together, with one acting as a timekeeper. Dubbed Frogmore Stew about 1948 by Richard Gay who owned a fish company on the island, the name is interchangeable with the Low Country Boil. Great for large holiday meals!

...

Low Country Yuca

Courtesy of Lou Veiga

8 cloves of garlic, minced
1/2 cup olive oil
1/8 tsp. fresh minced oregano (optional)
1/8 tsp. salt
1 lb. shrimp, shelled and deveined
1 cup chopped parsley
1 to 2 Tbsp. fresh lime juice

18 oz. frozen yuca
6 slices crispy bacon, cut into pieces (optional garnish)

Bring a large saucepan of salted water to a boil. Add the frozen yuca. Cook until the yuca centers are fork-tender (about 20 minutes). Drain water and keep yuca warm.

Add the olive oil to a large skillet and bring to medium-low heat. When the oil reaches its aromatic point, add garlic. Sauté for 15 seconds.

Add the shrimp. Sauté on medium heat, stirring lightly until the shrimp curl, about 5 minutes.

Remove the skillet from the heat and add the parsley, the oregano, the salt, and the lime juice. Mix thoroughly.

Place the cooked yuca on a warm serving platter. Pour the skillet contents over the yuca. Garnish with bacon bits.

Serves 4.

Two regionally distinct dishes merge in this newly created dish. Gambas al Ajillo is a Spanish favorite and it meets Low Country Shrimp and Grits, with cassava or yuca substituting for traditional grits.

American Beach African Americans

Northeast Florida African Americans needed a place for recreation near the beachfront during times of segregation. As a result, American Beach was established on Amelia Island in 1935. Abraham Lincoln Lewis, president of the Pension Bureau of the Afro-American Life Insurance Company, was its founder. He wanted it to be a place to relax for all Americans. Born in Madison County, Lewis is considered Florida's first African American millionaire, a generous man who contributed to many institutions. American Beach was listed on the National Register of Historic Places in 2002.

...

He Shorty's Pigs' Feet

Courtesy of Marsha Dean Phelts

12 pigs' feet, split in half lengthwise and well washed
2 cups white vinegar
2 Tbsp. salt
1 Tbsp. pepper

Barbeque Sauce:
1 quart ketchup
1 pint yellow mustard
1 Tbsp. salt
1/4 cup crushed red pepper flakes
2 Tbsp. chili powder
1 Tbsp. garlic powder
1/4 cup sugar
1/4 cup white vinegar

Place cleaned pigs' feet in a heavy 12-quart stockpot. Cover with water and 2 cups of vinegar. Add salt and pepper, bring to a full boil, lower heat to medium, and cook for 2 hours.

Prepare sauce by mixing all ingredients together.

Preheat oven to 300°F.

Remove pigs' feet from pot, coat each one in the special barbecue sauce, and arrange in a single layer in a roasting pan. Bake 2 hours uncovered, or until tender, basting frequently. Serves 4–6.

"He Shorty's Pigs' Feet" by Samuel Lee Thompson in *The American Beach Cookbook*, by Marsha Dean Phelts. Gainesville: University Press of Florida, 2008, pp. 45. Reprinted with permission of the University Press of Florida.

Samuel Lee Johnson was dubbed "He Shorty" by cookbook author Marsha Dean Phelts' young son. Six-year-old Kyle Michael Dean found it easier to refer to refer to Johnson and his wife as He and She Shorty, acknowledging their stature and also the warmth of family friendships.

A former Navy man, Johnson did the daily household cooking as well as cooking for special occasions. The Johnson home, a two-story house with wide porches on both levels and a huge backyard, was often the setting for parties.

"And he could cook anything—he had a wide range. He once served Queen Elizabeth!" said Dean Phelts.

...

Red Rice

Courtesy of Caulette Booth

16 oz. parboiled rice
6 oz. diced smoked sausage
6 slices bacon
1 16-oz. can tomato sauce
1 16-oz. can diced tomatoes
1 6-oz. can tomato paste
1 stalk celery, diced
1 medium onion, diced
1 small green pepper, diced
1 Tbsp. brown sugar
1 tsp. salt
Pepper to taste
1 clove garlic, diced
Water, 32 oz. (2 16-oz. cans full)

In a 5-quart saucepan cook bacon until crispy.

Remove bacon from pan but leave drippings for sauté.

On medium heat, sauté sausage, diced celery, diced onions, and diced green peppers until soft, about 3–4 minutes.

Stir in tomato sauce, diced tomatoes, and tomato paste until paste is well dissolved.

Stir in remaining ingredients (brown sugar, minced garlic, bacon, salt and pepper, and rice), increase heat to high, and bring to a boil.

Reduce heat to low and cover pot for 15 minutes. Stir rice, evenly working all ingredients, cover and continue cooking until rice is soft.

Red Rice is a Gullah Geechee classic served throughout the southeastern United States. In St. Johns County, the rural settlement of Armstrong is the southernmost point of the Gullah Geechee Heritage Corridor. A new and noteworthy contribution to Gullah Geechee culture is a beautiful cookbook called Bress 'N' Nyam: Gullah Geechee Recipes from a Sixth-Generation Farmer, by Matthew Raiford. This home cook is part of the community, though Booth moved from the Low Country and now lives in Baltimore, Maryland.

Minorcan and Old St. Augustine Recipes

...

Fromajardis Cheese Cakes

Pie Dough:
2 cups all-purpose flour
1 tsp. salt
1/8 tsp. nutmeg
2/3 cup chilled Crisco shortening
2 Tbsp. chilled butter
4 Tbsp. water

Filling:
1/2 lb. aged cheddar cheese
4 eggs, well beaten
1/8 tsp. salt
1/4 tsp. cayenne pepper (or less, to taste)
4 Tbsp. melted butter

In a bowl, sift together flour, salt, and nutmeg. In a second bowl, place the shortening and butter. Cut half of the shortening and butter into the flour mixture with a pastry blender or two knives, blending until it resembles cornmeal. Add the remaining shortening and butter and blend until the mixture forms pea-sized balls. Sprinkle it with water and blend lightly until dough gathers into a smooth ball. Place dough in waxed paper and chill it in the refrigerator while preparing the filling.

Grate cheese; beat in eggs, salt, and pepper. Roll chilled dough thin. Cut into five-inch rounds. On a half of each round, cut a cross.

Place one tablespoon of cheese on uncut half of dough circle. Fold to make a half circle; pinch edges together. Brush with melted butter. Bake in 375°F oven 20 minutes or until golden brown. Cheese will puff up through the cross. Makes about 15. Serve with Florida orange wine.

. . .

Peach Jam Cake

1 cup white raisins, soaked in peach brandy
1 cup butter or margarine
2 cups sugar
3 eggs, separated
1 cup peach jam
3 1/2 cups flour
1 1/2 tsp. baking powder
1/2 tsp. salt
1 tsp. cinnamon
1 tsp. nutmeg
1 tsp. allspice
1 tsp. ginger
1 cup buttermilk
1 tsp. baking soda
1 cup chopped pecans

Place raisins in brandy and let stand overnight. Cream butter and sugar until light. Add egg yolks; mix well. Add jam and beat until smooth. Sift together twice the flour, salt, baking powder, and spices. Stir baking soda into buttermilk and add to creamed mixture alternately with the flour, stirring to blend well each time. Toss nuts and raisins in a little flour, fold into cake mixture.

Beat egg whites until stiff and fold in. Pour into oiled tube pan and bake at 350°F for 45 minutes or until cake tests done.

Stove-Top Chicken Pilau

(Pronounced "Chicken Pur-lo")

4 slices bacon
1 Tbsp. green pepper, chopped
1 onion, chopped
1 28-oz. can tomatoes
1 cup okra, thinly sliced *or* half of one 10-oz. pkg. frozen cut okra
    thawed
1 Tbsp. sugar
1 tsp. salt
1 cup water
1/4 tsp. ground red pepper
1 small hot green or Datil pepper, chopped
1 cup long grain rice
2 cups cooked chicken, cut in cubes
1 Tbsp. chopped parsley

Fry bacon in skillet until crisp. Set aside to drain on paper towel. In bacon drippings, sauté onion and green pepper until tender. Add canned tomatoes, okra, sugar, salt, water, red pepper, hot green pepper, uncooked rice, and chicken. Cover tightly; simmer until rice is cooked, about 25 minutes. Serve in a colorful bowl, topped with crumbled bacon and parsley. (Note: This recipe is peppery. It is wise to start with half the quantities given for the ground red pepper and hot green or Datil pepper and adjust the amounts to suit your taste.) Serves 6.

• • •

Minorcan Christmas Candy

1 cup freshly grated coconut
2 cups sugar
2 1/2 cups coconut milk
3 Tbsp. white Karo syrup

Stir coconut, sugar, and milk to blend well; add syrup. Over very low heat, cook, stirring constantly until mixture becomes thick and heavy. Drop in small teaspoonfuls onto waxed paper and allow to harden. (Note: If prepared coconut is used, soak 1/4 cup coconut in warm milk for one hour, then strain it to get coconut milk.) Makes about 60 candies.

Minorcan Clam Chowder

Courtesy of Mary Ellen Masters

Makes 15 gallons

15 lbs. frozen chopped clams

3 46-oz. cans of clam juice, adding more as needed when reheating chowder

15 lbs. Spanish onions

1 No. 10 can (105 oz.) tomato puree, along with 1 28-oz. can tomato puree

2 No. 10 cans (105 oz. each) crushed tomatoes

2½ lbs. salt pork, diced

4 green bell peppers

2 celery stalks; if leaves are bitter, don't use. If not, use inner leaves.

20 lbs. red potatoes, unpeeled and diced

Salt and pepper to taste

Datil peppers to taste

½ cup dried thyme

½ cup dried Italian seasoning

¼ cup marjoram

In a large pot, fry the diced salt pork until it turns brown, then add the onions, green peppers, and celery that have been ground in a food processor. Cook until tender. Add the chopped bell peppers and celery and sauté until tender. Add both tomatoes—pureed and crushed.

Boil the potatoes in a separate pot until they start to soften. Add to the larger pot. Next, add the clam juice. Finally, add the clams. Simmer until all the seasonings meld. Check for salt content and add it and pepper according to taste.

Datil peppers are also added according to taste for heat level. Remove the stems but do not remove the seeds, then grind them in a food processor and add to the chowder.

Spicy and satisfying, this chowder recipe was shared after the cook catered a wedding feast where it was featured, so the measurements were on her mind. For more than 25 years, Masters' chowder has been the star of the St. Ambrose Catholic Church festivals in Elkton, Florida. At the church's 139th spring festival in 2022, Masters and her crew served more than 160 gallons before running out of it after 1½ hours.

First Coast Filipinos

More than 33,000 Filipinos make Jacksonville home, and they represent the city's largest Asian population. The first wave of Filipinos came during the 1940s as a result of their large increase in enlistment in the U.S. Navy during World War II. The Naval Air Station Jacksonville was established in 1940. By the 1950s, 90 percent of the Filipino population in north Florida was linked to the military. Today's community includes those with military backgrounds and their families as well as others who found an attractive way of life in Duval County.

. . .

Chicken Adobo

Courtesy of Marie Espedido

1 cup white vinegar
¼ cup soy sauce
1 whole garlic bulb, smashed and peeled
2 tsp. Kosher salt
1 tsp. ground pepper
1 bay leaf
2 lbs. chicken thighs or drumsticks
1 Tbsp. canola oil
1 cup water

Mix vinegar, soy sauce, garlic, Kosher salt, ground pepper, and bay leaf in a large bowl. Then add chicken, coating it evenly. Cover and refrigerate for 30 to 60 minutes. Drain and save the marinade. Pat the chicken dry.

In a large skillet, heat oil over medium-high heat. Stir in water and marinade and bring to a boil. Reduce the heat and simmer chicken in a skillet, uncovered, until chicken is no longer pink and sauce is reduced, about 20–25 minutes.

This recipe comes from the home cook's mother's kitchen in Manila, the Philippines. Her husband Alvin Espedido works in the medical field and was recruited to Jacksonville by a U.S. company. The dish is made regularly at their Jacksonville home today for its simplicity and taste.

. . .

Salmon with Salted Black Beans

Courtesy of Felisa Recon Franklin

4 salmon fillets, each 6 to 8 oz.
Salt and pepper to taste
2 Tbsp. neutral oil

Sauce:
2 Tbsp. salted black beans, rinsed
3 Tbsp. hoisin sauce
Water, as needed
15 to 20 cherry tomatoes, halved
1 onion, thinly sliced
5 cloves garlic, minced
1 Tbsp. minced ginger
3 or 4 green onions, sliced in ¼ inch pieces, for garnish

Note: Salted black beans, sometimes called fermented black beans, are sold in cans at local Asian markets.

Pat dry the salmon fillets dry with a paper towel, then sprinkle them with a pinch of salt and lots of black pepper. Put the oil in a skillet, and fry the fish over medium heat, about 2–3 minutes each side. Set aside.

To make the sauce, pour 2–3 tablespoons of cooking oil into a skillet and use medium heat.

Add the minced ginger and thinly sliced onion to the pan. Toss until onions become translucent (about 3 minutes).

Add the garlic. Toss for 1 minute.

Next, add the black beans and cherry tomatoes. Sauté until the tomatoes are soft.

Add water, about a tablespoon at a time (up to 3 tablespoons), to lighten the consistency of the sauce, if desired.

Taste the sauce and adjust seasonings if needed by adding more water, hoisin sauce, and/or salt.

Pour the black bean sauce while hot onto the plate of fried salmon. Top the dish with sliced green onions and serve.

Felisa Recon was born in Rosario, Batangas, Philippines. She and her husband Michael Franklin met while teaching at a United Nations refugee processing center in Morong, Bataan. They married in 1987 and moved to Jacksonville from Chicago in 2004. Apart from teaching, she has worked in human resources and for the IRS.

...

Pinoy Fruit Salad

Courtesy of Felisa Recon Franklin

Fruit cocktail, in a 30-oz. can. Use only 15 oz.

Nestle table cream, 7.6-fluid-oz. can. Use only half or 3.6 oz.

Note: Label may show "media crema lite"; usually available in the Latino section of major supermarkets.

Condensed milk, 14-oz. can. Use only 1/2 or 7 oz.

A fresh apple, cut into small cubes (to match the size of the fruit in the fruit cocktail)

Maraschino cherries, about 10 pieces

A pinch of salt

Empty the fruit cocktail into a strainer. Strain for 2 hours or overnight in the refrigerator. Remove as much liquid as possible. Cut up the apple into small cubes. Add to the fruit cocktail in a bowl. Prepare the liquid component by mixing in a separate bowl the condensed milk and Nestle table cream thoroughly so there are no lumps. Add a pinch of salt. Mix the liquid with the fruit. Refrigerate for about 3 hours. Stir in the maraschino cherries before serving.

Pinoy is a popular name for Filipinos (the people) or Philippines (the country).

Northeast Florida Specialties

...

Scallops St. Augustine

1/2 lb. scallops, fresh or frozen

2 Tbsp. margarine or butter

1 Tbsp. olive oil
1 tsp. marjoram
1/2 tsp. salt
1/4 tsp. white pepper
1 cup sliced mushrooms
2 Tbsp. sliced green onion
1/2 cup sherry wine
1/4 cup white wine
2 Tbsp. cornstarch
2 servings cooked, seasoned wild rice

Thaw scallops if frozen. Rinse scallops to remove any remaining shell particles; cut large scallops in half. Melt margarine with oil in 10-inch frying pan over medium-high heat. Add scallops, marjoram, salt, and pepper. Cook 2 to 3 minutes until scallops begin to turn opaque. Remove from pan with slotted spoon and set aside. In the same pan, cook mushrooms and onions 3 to 4 minutes. Add sherry and white wine; cook until volume is reduced by half. Add cornstarch and cook until thickened, stirring continuously. Reduce heat, replace scallops in pan, and cook 3 minutes longer or until scallops are done. Serve immediately over hot cooked wild rice. Serves 2.

Surfers on the Atlantic

Surfers are eating at places along the beaches where they are welcome—still a little salty and sandy. A preference for healthy, fresh food after surfing sessions—possibly born of fresh fish cooked above driftwood fires on the beach and fresh coconut water—translates to food trucks, taco stands, and small, casual, independently owned restaurants. Tastes run to handheld, fresh, light foods. Fish tacos with Baja sauce, burritos, and a host of vegetarian sandwiches are the draw.

Lemon–Baked Chicken with Spiced Peaches

1 3-lb. broiler-fryer chicken, quartered
1 Tbsp. flour
1 tsp. Accent
1/2 tsp. salt
1/2 tsp. pepper
1/2 tsp. paprika
1 Tbsp. butter or margarine
3 Tbsp. lemon or lime juice

Place chicken in shallow baking dish. Combine flour, Accent, salt, pepper, and paprika; sprinkle over chicken. Dot with butter. Bake uncovered at 375°F for 30 minutes. Sprinkle with lemon juice; bake 20 minutes longer. (Only 200 calories per serving!) Serve with spiced peaches.

...

Spiced Peaches

1 29-oz. can cling peach halves
1 tsp. whole cloves
1/3 cup brown sugar
1/4 cup lemon or lime juice

Drain peach syrup into saucepan. Stud peach halves with half the cloves; set aside. Bring syrup and remaining cloves to a boil; boil rapidly until reduced to half a cup. Add sugar, lemon juice, and peaches; bring to a boil. Remove from heat. Serve warm with chicken. Serves 4.

...

Southern Barbecued Chicken

3 dressed young broilers, split
2 Tbsp. ketchup
2 Tbsp. vinegar
1/2 tsp. dry mustard
1 Tbsp. lemon or lime juice
1/4 tsp. Tabasco sauce
2 Tbsp. Worcestershire sauce
2 Tbsp. water

5 Tbsp. melted butter
¹/₂ tsp. paprika

Rub each broiler half with salt, pepper, and melted butter. Place on broiler rack, skin facedown, and cook under moderate heat until brown and almost tender. Turn and cook other side. Mix ingredients and use to baste chicken frequently during broiling. Serves 6.

• • •

Barbecued Shrimp

2 lbs. raw, large shrimp
¹/₃ cup minced onion
3 Tbsp. olive oil
1 cup ketchup
¹/₃ cup lemon juice
2 Tbsp. brown sugar
¹/₂ cup hot water
2 tsp. prepared mustard
2 Tbsp. Worcestershire sauce
¹/₄ tsp. salt
1 tsp. chili sauce

In heavy pan, sauté onion in olive oil until transparent. Peel and devein shrimp. Add remaining ingredients except shrimp to onion in pan. Turn heat to low; cover and simmer 10 minutes. Place shrimp on broiling platter; cover with sauce. With shrimp 6 inches below broiler, broil about 6 minutes or until shrimp are cooked. Turn once. Serve hot with remaining sauce. Serves 4.

• • •

Roast Pork, Spanish Style

6 lb. pork loin roast
2 cloves garlic
1 tsp. salt
¹/₄ tsp. pepper
4 Tbsp. oregano
²/₃ cup fresh lime juice

Cut garlic into slivers; make slits all over the roast and insert garlic.

Combine salt, pepper, and oregano. Rub this over the meat. Place fat side up on a rack pan in preheated 450°F oven; immediately reduce heat to 350°F and cook uncovered 30–35 minutes per pound. If a meat thermometer is used, it should read 185°F when finished. When pork begins to brown, baste frequently with lime juice. (This roast has slight garlic flavor with a crisp, tart crust.) Serve with spiced crabapples. Serves 8–10.

Florida Vegetables

...

Red-and-White Tomato Molded Salad

1 envelope gelatin
1/2 cup cold tomato juice
11/4 cups hot tomato juice
1/2 tsp. salt
1 Tbsp. lemon juice

Soften gelatin in 2 tablespoons cold tomato juice. Stir in remaining cold, then hot tomato juice. When dissolved, mix in salt and lemon juice. Pour into oiled loaf pan; refrigerate until almost firm; add egg salad layer (see below). Chill until set; unmold and serve with mayonnaise mixed with mashed avocado. Serves 8.

Egg Salad Layer:
1 envelope gelatin
1/2 cup cold water
1 tsp. salt
1 Tbsp. lemon juice
1/2 tsp. Worcestershire sauce
1/2 tsp. pepper
1/4 cup pimiento, finely chopped
4 hard-cooked eggs, chopped
2 tsp. onion, grated
1/2 cup celery, finely chopped
1/4 cup green pepper, finely chopped
1 Tbsp. celery seed
1/4 cup mayonnaise

Soften gelatin in cold water. Place in top of double boiler and heat until dissolved, stirring slowly. Add salt, lemon juice, Worcestershire, and pepper. Cool. Add mayonnaise and remaining ingredients, stirring until well blended.

• • •

Broccoli Soufflé with Cheese Sauce

1 Tbsp. butter or margarine, divided
3 Tbsp. cornstarch
1 cup beef bouillon
2 tsp. lemon juice
1/2 tsp. salt
1/4 tsp. Tabasco sauce
1/2 tsp. nutmeg
4 egg yolks
1/3 cup grated Parmesan cheese
2 Tbsp. chopped scallions
1 10-oz. package frozen chopped broccoli, or fresh broccoli, cooked
5 egg whites
1/2 tsp. cream of tartar

Melt 3 tablespoons butter in pan; blend in cornstarch. Gradually stir in bouillon. Cook, stirring constantly, until mixture thickens and comes to a boil. Remove from heat. Stir in lemon juice, salt, Tabasco, and nutmeg. Beat egg yolks in small bowl and stir in a little hot sauce. Stir into remaining sauce and add grated cheese. Melt remaining 1 tablespoon butter in skillet; add scallions and cook until tender. Add thawed broccoli; stir over moderately high heat until moisture evaporates, then add to sauce.

Beat egg whites with cream of tartar until stiff but not dry. Stir about one-quarter of the beaten egg whites into the broccoli sauce; mix well. Fold in remaining whites, mixing as little as possible. Turn into buttered 1 1/2-quart soufflé dish and sprinkle top with more grated Parmesan cheese. Bake in 375°F oven 35–40 minutes, until top is puffed and browned. (Center will be moist; for a drier, firmer center, bake until a knife inserted in center comes out clean.) Serve with cheese sauce. Serves 6.

Cheese Sauce

2 Tbsp. butter
1/2 tsp. salt
1/2 tsp. dry mustard
2 Tbsp. flour
1/4 tsp. Tabasco
1 1/2 cups milk
1 cup cheddar cheese, shredded

Melt butter in pan; blend in flour and seasonings. Stir in milk. Cook, stirring constantly, until mixture thickens and comes to a boil. Cook 2 minutes longer, stirring constantly. Add cheese; stir until melted.

• • •

Southern Corn Pudding

2 cups milk
2 cups corn, cut from the cob
1/4 cup melted butter
1 Tbsp. sugar
1 tsp. salt
1/4 tsp. pepper
1 egg, well beaten

Combine milk and corn in saucepan and heat. Beat eggs; set aside. Add to milk and corn the butter, sugar, and seasonings. Pour a little corn mixture over the beaten eggs. Beat this, then return to corn mixture. Stir and cook for several minutes. Turn into a greased casserole and bake in 350°F oven about 45 minutes, or until pudding sets. Serves 6.

A real old-fashioned Southern dinner would include fried chicken with gravy, rice, corn pudding, sliced ripe tomato salad, hot biscuits with guava jelly, and for dessert, a richly frosted Lane Cake or homemade peach ice cream. Corn pudding and barbecued chicken were traditional partners at political gatherings in the early South.

···

Hot Bollos,
Afro-Cuban Style

2 lbs. dried black-eyed peas
1/4 tsp. pepper
3 cloves garlic
3 Tbsp. scraped onion
1 tsp. salt
Seeds of small, dried hot pepper
Water
Olive or cooking oil

Wash and pick peas; soak overnight in cold water. Rub peas against sides of a sieve until hulls come off. Wash again, scooping off hulls that float on top. Drain peas, mix with other ingredients except cooking oil. Chop in food processor using fine blade. Add enough water to make a thick paste, form into small balls. Fry balls in deep cooking oil at 375°F until golden brown. Serve as a hot appetizer. (Recipe borrowed from Cubans in Key West, where hot Bollos were sold on street corners, much like they were once sold in the streets of Havana.)

Bollos are one of countless types of fritters introduced in the New World by Africans. They are featured in the cuisine of the U.S. South as well as countries throughout the rest of the Caribbean and the Americas where plantation economies flourished.

Desserts

···

Frosty Lemon Milk Sherbet

1 cup evaporated milk
1/2 cup sugar
2 cups water
1 Tbsp. fresh mint, chopped
1/2 cup fresh lemon juice
1/4 tsp. lemon rind, grated
2 tsp. vanilla
1/2 tsp. ground mace

Lemon gives a tropical taste to Frosty Lemon Milk Sherbet.

¹/₂ tsp. salt
Grated fresh lemon rind

Pour evaporated milk into freezing tray. Place in freezer and chill until frozen around sides, about 1 hour. Combine sugar, water, and fresh mint in pan. Bring to boiling point; boil 2–3 minutes. Remove from heat; cool. Stir in lemon juice, lemon rind, vanilla, ground mace, and salt. Turn into freezing tray and freeze to a mush, about 1 hour. Whip partially frozen evaporated milk until thick and fluffy. Gradually beat in frozen lemon mixture. Return to two freezing trays and freeze until firm. Garnish with grated lemon rind. Serves 8.

. . .

Papaya Nut Pie

1 cup orange juice
1 Tbsp. cornstarch
¹/₄ cup sugar
Juice of 1 lemon
¹/₂ tsp. ground ginger
1¹/₂ cups diced papaya, fresh or canned
9-inch pie shell, baked
Whipped cream
Toasted coconut

Blend orange juice, cornstarch, sugar, lemon, and ginger; heat slowly in pan, stirring constantly until thick and clear. Cool slightly. Pour over papaya cubes placed in baked pie shell. Refrigerate and chill well. Swirl whipped cream on top and sprinkle with toasted coconut before serving. Makes 1 pie.

. . .

Banana–Rum Pudding with Meringue

1 cup milk
1¹/₃ cup cornstarch
1 cup sugar, divided
¹/₄ tsp. salt, divided
3 egg yolks, beaten
1 tsp. vanilla

1 tsp. rum flavoring
26 small vanilla wafers
3 large bananas
1 egg white

Mix cornstarch with 2/3 cup sugar and 1/2 teaspoon salt. Scald milk in top of double boiler; pour slowly over cornstarch mixture. Cook over boiling water, stirring constantly, until mixture thickens. Cover; cook 15 minutes, stirring occasionally. Add hot mixture very slowly to beaten egg yolks, stirring constantly. Return mixture to double boiler; cook 2 minutes. Cool; add vanilla and rum flavoring. In 1½-quart casserole, place alternate layers of wafers, bananas, and pudding, ending with pudding. Add 1/4 teaspoon salt to egg whites; beat until foamy. Gradually add 1/3 cup sugar, beating until soft peaks form. Pile egg whites on pudding; bake in 350°F oven for 10–15 minutes or until light brown. Chill. Serves 6.

Guava Shells with Cream Cheese

One of the most delicious—and wonderfully simple—desserts in Florida is a gift from Spanish settlers. Pretty pink guava shells are sold canned in most Latin American grocery stores. Simply open the can, serve them with or without the spicy juice, with a generous wedge of cream cheese. If you like, add a very salty crisp cracker for flavor contrast. A compliment-winner.

Florida Gold Coast

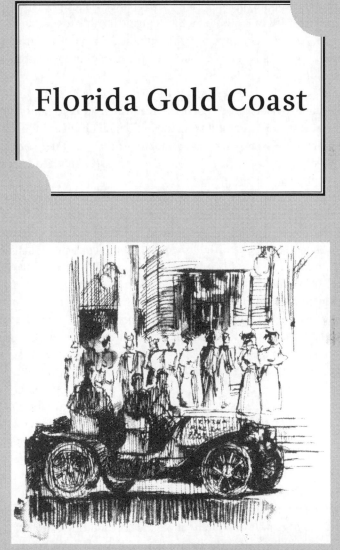

Excitement was high in 1908 when the first automobile traveled from Jacksonville to Miami in five days.

We know native people called the Tequesta lived near Biscayne Bay in 1513, because Ponce de León reported seeing them when he sailed into the Bay and discovered Cape Florida. Their territory spanned to today's north Broward County and even central Palm Beach County. Some of the bones and broken tools found there date back to 400 to 1400 A.D.

At the mouth of the then clear blue Miami River, a group of missionaries settled in 1568. When British control came to Florida in 1763, about 300 natives moved to Cuba with the Spanish. Later, in 1836, soldiers built Fort Dallas there to block Seminole trading with Cuba and other islands of the West Indies.

But the barrier islands were where the action was. A handful of people attempted to start coconut and avocado plantations among the mangroves, sea grape, and scrub palmetto of Miami Beach in 1882. Insects plagued the workers; rats and rabbits ate the young tree shoots. By 1890 it was given up as a failure. Happily, enough trees survived to make Miami Beach a palm-fringed island.

In Miami, meanwhile, William Brickell built a home on the river's south shore while Julia Tuttle settled on the north side. She put Miami on the map the day she cut an orange blossom, packed it in damp cotton, and sent it to Henry Flagler in north Florida. This ambitious woman had been urging him to extend his railroad to Miami, but he ignored her until the winter of 1894, when a hard freeze killed north Florida citrus.

The blossoms lured Flagler southward, where he verified that Miami was indeed basking in the sunshine, far from icy breezes. He accepted gifts of land from Julia Tuttle and other residents, and built his railroad. It brought guests to his hotels: a new wooden Royal Palm Hotel in Miami, the Ponce de León in St. Augustine, and the Royal Poinciana in Palm Beach.

While millionaires enjoyed bay breezes at Flagler's Royal Palm Hotel, Miami Beach began to stir. Some dredging was done and the longest wooden bridge in the nation was begun by John S. Collins, then stopped when funds ran out. Millionaire promoter Carl F. Fisher of Indianapolis loaned him $50,000 with 200 acres of land as security, and the bridge was completed.

Fisher's promotional genius lured the wealthy south, persuaded them to invest, and began the development of land and building of hotels.

In the early 1920s, people by the millions came to Miami and Miami Beach, eager to make a fortune in the fantastic Florida land boom that peaked in 1925. To the Southerners who had made it their home were added Latino, Caribbean, Central and South Americans as well as people from industrial centers in the north and Midwest. All brought their food preferences with them, laying a foundation for Miami's contemporary vibrant food scene.

When, in 1926, the railroad broke down and a sunken ship blocked the harbor, preventing delivery of tons of building supplies, the boom went bust. The final misfortune was the great hurricane of September 18, 1926. It wiped out homes and businesses, killed hundreds, and pushed water from the ocean over to the bay.

Tourism—based on the new idea of package vacations for moderate-income families—revived the area and brought back a prosperity that has seldom faltered since. Air conditioning extended the vacation season from winter throughout the summer. And the population continued to climb.

In 1973, when seven and a half years of Freedom Flights from Cuba ended, some 260,000 Cuban refugees had reached Miami. Desperate Cubans continued making the risky voyage in small boats and flimsy rafts—even inner tube rafts—until by 1994, Dade County's total population soared to nearly two million. Southwest Eighth Street became Little Havana and Spanish was the language of choice.

Miami continues to grow, with tourists from the Americas and Europe making Miami International Airport one of the busiest in the country. In downtown Miami, a people mover whisks visitors to theaters, restaurants, shopping malls, and museums. In Miami Beach, picturesque hotels built in the thirties form the nucleus of an Art Deco district where sidewalk jazz concerts enliven the night. The Miami Dolphins football team has its own stadium, the Hard Rock Stadium, seating 65,326, in north Miami-Dade County.

Once a sleepy Southern town, Miami is now home to long-time U.S. residents from various parts of our nation as well as Colombians, Peruvians, Venezuelans, Brazilians, Argentines, Panamanians, Puerto Ricans, Dominicans, Nicaraguans, Salvadoreans, Haitians, Jamaicans, Cubans, and many other Caribbean islanders and Latin Americans. These are just a few of the cultures thriving alongside one another in South Florida. It has become a major metropolis—the Gateway to Latin America. Miami-Dade County is the state's largest county with 2,742,833 residents in 2022.

One of the nation's largest Jewish communities began growing on Miami Beach; by 1947, nearly half the permanent population was Jewish. Cuban refugees fleeing Castro's regime flowed into Miami by the hundreds of thousands. The imprint of both groups is reflected in the communities, and especially in the many fine Jewish and Cuban restaurants in South Florida. Other immigrants followed.

Follow the beach from Miami Beach north and you reach Fort Lauderdale, the boating capital of the world, with 135 miles of waterways. Here is Port Everglades, the deepest harbor on Florida's east coast. The city was named to honor Major William Lauderdale, who commanded the local fort during the Seminole War.

The wide, white beach continues north to Palm Beach. Great mansions drowse in the beautiful seaside resort where Flagler built his hotel for millionaires in 1893. Addison Mizner's architectural touch remains, revealed in the mellow-toned red tile roofs and Spanish arches of the aging but still beautiful mansions. Worth Avenue is still one of the world's most beautiful streets, with many elegant shops displaying and selling fine wares. Though it remains a favorite spot with many U.S. socialites, inflation has struck and many of the great homes of Palm Beach have become museums or have been replaced by commercial buildings. But the food in elegant Palm Beach restaurants is still among the world's best.

Northward, the beach curves inward beside Fort Pierce, Melbourne, and to John F. Kennedy Space Center. From the Center, the first moon landing by Apollo 11 was made in 1969, followed by six moon shots. In 1981, the first manned space shuttle launches were made. Next came the launch of the first five-member crew in 1983. In 1986, disaster struck

Food Forests in Urban School Yards

The Education Fund has established 51 eco-labs in designated public elementary schools across Miami-Dade County. The labs, also known as food forests, span a quarter acre or more at sites and are filled with fruits, vegetables, and herbs in the form of trees, bushes, and ground cover. Plants are chosen for the climate zone and students' native homeland diets. Students thrive academically and in other ways along with the produce. To date, more than 232,000 harvest bags have gone home with students, and parents often request more produce.

when the space shuttle *Challenger* exploded after takeoff and all seven astronauts were killed, including a teacher who planned to teach from space.

Two years later the space program resumed. Today, rocket-powered probes venture deep into space, exploring distant planets and expanding scientists' knowledge of the universe. Weather satellites stationed in space have revolutionized weather reporting and communications, and scientific experiments in space enable teams to spend long periods in spacecrafts with scientists from other countries, including Russia.

South Florida's food is a world unto itself. The nation's only true subtropical area produces exotic mangoes, avocados, limes, lychee nuts, coconuts, as well as a full array of winter vegetables, a large portion of which is grown in the Homestead and Redlands area. Seafood is plentiful, with stone crabs, lobster, red snapper, and mackerel among the favorites.

Spanish Specialties
Cuban and Spanish Specialties

. . .

Frijoles Negros a la Cubano
(Cuban Black Beans)

2 cups (1 lb.) black beans
Water, sufficient to cover beans
½ tsp. salt, or to taste
1 clove garlic, cut in half
2 Tbsp. olive oil
3 cloves garlic, mashed
1 bay leaf
1 green pepper, minced
1 onion, chopped
1 Tbsp. cider vinegar
Salt, pepper to taste
Fluffy white rice

Wash and pick beans. Place in covered pot with enough water to stand one inch above beans. Soak overnight. Add salt and garlic halves and cook beans until tender. Meanwhile, to make *sofrito*, heat oil in heavy frying pan and add mashed garlic, bay leaf, green pepper, and onion. Lower heat to simmer and cook 5 minutes. Add vinegar and salt to taste. Mix with beans and reheat until hot. Serve with fluffy white rice. Serves 6.

• • •

Eggs in Spanish Sauce

1 29-oz. can tomatoes
1 sliced onion
1 tsp. sugar
1/4 tsp. Tabasco
1/4 tsp. salt
1/8 tsp. ground cloves
1/2 bay leaf
1 Tbsp. butter or margarine
2 Tbsp. flour
2 cups cooked rice
6 eggs
1/4 cup grated cheddar cheese

Combining rice with eggs in this fashion is popular in old Spain as well as in Latin American countries.

Simmer tomatoes, onion, sugar, Tabasco, salt, cloves, and bay leaf in saucepan about 10 minutes. Remove bay leaf. Blend butter and flour together. Add to tomato mixture. Cook, stirring constantly, until thickened. Spread rice in greased shallow 2 1/2-quart casserole, making 6 hollows in it with a tablespoon. Break an egg into each nest. Carefully pour sauce over all. Sprinkle with cheese. Bake in 350°F oven 20 minutes or until the eggs are firm. Serves 6.

• • •

Spanish-Cuban Thanksgiving Turkey

Courtesy of Glenna Veiga

Along with her father and sister, Carmen Ballesteros-Martin immigrated to Punta San Juan, Camaguay, Cuba, during the 1920s from Ledesma, Spain. She lived, worked, and married there, becoming an Echevarria. In 1960, she and her husband went into exile in the United States. The legacy of her Spanish-Cuban cooking lives on in the foods she taught her family to prepare. Her turkey recipe will replace any other.

Buy a fresh (not frozen) turkey. Its size depends on the number of people you are serving, so check the packaging instructions for appropriate weight and cooking time. Keep the cooking/packaging instructions.

For Day 1 (Tuesday):
A fresh turkey
A large bottle of white vinegar
A cheesecloth, or thin kitchen towel
A large nonreactive platter on which to place the turkey during its marinating time

Rinse the turkey under cool water and pat dry. Place it on the platter. Then douse the turkey (inside and out) with the vinegar. Saturate the cheesecloth as well. Cover the turkey with the saturated cheesecloth, then put clear plastic wrap around it and refrigerate for 24 hours.

For Day 2 (Wednesday):
Juice from 3–4 Persian limes
4–6 garlic cloves, minced
1/2 – 3/4 cup olive oil
Salt and pepper

Take the turkey out of the refrigerator and gently wash off all of the vinegar, then pat dry. In a measuring cup, add the lime juice, minced garlic cloves, salt, and pepper. This is the marinade. Put the turkey back on the platter, then pour the marinade over it. Cover with the cheesecloth, then plastic wrap, and refrigerate for another day.

On Thanksgiving Day:
The marinated turkey
A meat thermometer
A turkey baster
Aluminum foil
A roasting pan

Preheat the oven to 450°F, then bake the bird in a roasting pan, uncovered, for about 15–20 minutes. This sears it and locks in the juices. Then cover the turkey loosely with aluminum foil. You may also wish to wrap aluminum foil around the ends of the drumsticks. Lower the heat, and cook according to the packaging instructions. Every 15–20 minutes, uncover the bird, and baste it, extracting the juices from the bottom of the pan, and squeezing it over the top and sides. Baste regularly to ensure moist meat.

About 15 minutes before the indicated cooking time is up, insert the meat thermometer and check the turkey's internal temperature. Again refer to the packaging/cooking instructions, which will tell you where to insert the thermometer, and what the temperature should be.

Once cooked, remove it from the oven, and allow 15 minutes to cool before carving. Prepare the gravy as you wait.

The Gravy
In a skillet, melt about ½ a stick of butter. Then, take a tablespoon of flour and gently sprinkle it into the skillet, while stirring the butter with a fork. This will make a paste. Add a generous amount of the pan drippings, along with some sherry or white wine for added aroma/flavor. If you like, add some B&B canned mushrooms. If the gravy is too salty or thick, add water or unsalted chicken broth until it has the consistency and flavor to your liking.

. . .

Malanga Fritters

Courtesy of Rosario Rosell

1 lb. taro root, peeled
1 egg
1 garlic clove
1 Tbsp. chopped parsley
1 tsp. salt
1 tsp. vinegar
Neutral oil for frying

Grate the taro and mix in a bowl with the other ingredients. Make sure the oil in a skillet is hot, then, using a teaspoon, take the batter and drop spoonfuls into the skillet. Watch them so you know when it's time to turn them once. Drain on paper towels and serve.

Created by Maria Josefa Sandoval de Rosell during the 1920s on the Las Batea Farm in Caney, Santiago, Cuba. Her daughter shared this classic fritter recipe from her Miami home. Malanga is closely related to the taro root and eddo corms, the last two more popular in Asian cooking. They are in the Araceae family and can be used interchangeably in recipes.

Oxtails with a Cuban–
Salvadorean Twist

Courtesy of Jenny Raun-Alonso

4½ lbs. oxtails
2 onions, chopped
3 scallions, chopped
5 garlic cloves, chopped
Water, just enough to cover the oxtails
4 cups beef broth
1½ cups crushed tomatoes
2 large carrots, cut into large chunks
8 small red potatoes, partially peeled and cut in quarters
½ tsp. ground cumin
2 envelopes of Sazon with Achiote
¼ cup fresh cilantro
Salt and pepper
All-purpose flour
Extra virgin olive oil
1 cup of red wine (one you would drink)

In a large pot, add oxtails, season with salt and pepper, add the onions, scallions, and garlic, and marinate at least 4 hours or overnight in the refrigerator, stirring occasionally.

On a separate plate place two cups of all-purpose flour, salt and pepper to taste, and mix together.

One by one dredge the oxtails in the mixture and place on a separate dish until all are out of the marinating pot.

In a deep pot, at 350°F, heat the olive oil and sauté the onions and garlic for about 2 minutes until clear, then remove from the pot and set aside.

Jenny Raun-Alonso enjoyed oxtails for lunch when she was growing up in San Salvador, El Salvador. Household cook Teresa Olivares made it along with fresh tortillas. The bowl of oxtail stew was topped with avocado slices as well as chopped cilantro. Sometimes hot sauce was added. She did not eat oxtails again until years later, when a Cuban version of the dish was served for lunch at her mother-in-law's house in Hialeah. Recalling her native version, Jenny succeeded in combing both heritages into one exceptional recipe.

Add another tablespoon of olive oil to the pot and start adding the oxtails, making sure to not crowd the pan. Sear each tail on all sides to keep the juices sealed. Remove the tails and set aside.

Return the onions and garlic to the pot and add the wine. Slowly stir the bottom of the pot to scrape the delicious pieces and seasonings left there. Add the cumin and the Sazon packages while mixing easily.

Add enough water to just cover the oxtails.

Add the crushed tomatoes and beef broth. Bring to a boil then simmer covered for about 1 hour and 30 minutes, stirring occasionally.

Add the carrots and potatoes. Cook for 30 minutes more or until everything is tender. Sprinkle fresh cilantro on top and serve with white rice.

Haitians

Haitians arrived at South Florida by boat in 1963 followed by larger populations fleeing the dictatorship of Baby Doc Duvalier by various means. Between 1977 and 1981, more than 70,000 Haitians came. Little Haiti was formed in the Miami neighborhoods of Lemon City and Little River. Today, Florida is home to more than half a million Haitians. Jacksonville has a Haitian community but South Florida has larger numbers. Their eateries are abundant. Their cuisine, while having commonalities with neighboring islands, distinguishes itself with its own seasonings including the use of star anise and the *Piman Bouk* pepper.

...

Haitian Roast Chicken
with Two Stuffings

1 Tbsp. butter plus 4 Tbsp. butter
1 garlic clove
1 cup soft breadcrumbs
1 Tbsp. lime juice
1 Tbsp. grated lime rind
1 tsp. brown sugar

1½ tsp. salt
¼ tsp. nutmeg
⅛ tsp. red pepper flakes
Black pepper to taste
5 ripe bananas, medium size
3½ to 4 lb. roasting chicken
1 cup chicken broth

Preheat oven to 350°F.

Place chopped bananas in a bowl and add 1 Tbsp. or more of lime juice, ½ tsp. salt, and pepper to taste. Toss and set aside.

In a skillet, melt 3 Tbsp. butter, then add peeled garlic clove for about 30 seconds. Remove and discard it. Add breadcrumbs, stirring until they are browned.

Take skillet off heat. Add 3 Tbsps. lime juice and rind, brown sugar, nutmeg, red pepper flakes, 1 tsp. salt, and then pepper to taste.

Rinse the chicken both inside and out and pat dry with paper towels. This step has been hailed as not necessary but I still do it.

Fill the breast cavity with bananas. Follow it with bread stuffing. Close the cavity with wooden toothpicks.

Use the rest of the butter to coat the chicken with a pastry brush. Place in a shallow roasting pan and roast for about one and a half hours, basting every 15 minutes or so.

Doneness test: pierce chicken thigh with knife point. If juices are pale yellow, it's done. If any pink, cook for another 5 to 10 minutes. Transfer to cutting board and let it rest for 5 minutes.

With a large spoon, remove stuffing and place in center of serving platter. Chicken pieces will surround it.

Bring the broth to boil and then lower to simmer. Add drippings from the roasting pan and cook for 2–3 minutes. Taste for seasoning and serve in a separate bowl.

I traveled to Haiti during the late 1980s and bought the Mountain Maid Best Made Cookbook, compiled by Amy Wolff at a Baptist Mission in the mountains outside the capital. Over time, I made a few small changes in methods. Sometimes, I use only a banana stuffing. This dish has been central to many happy meals in my home with company.

...

Arepas

Courtesy of Militza Garrillo

1 cup pre-cooked white corn flour. Most popular brands are Harina P.A.N. and Misia Juana. Similar to the flour used for polenta.
1/2 teaspoon of salt, a little more if desired
1 1/2 cups of water

In a bowl, mix the ingredients and knead for about 2–3 minutes. Allow the mixture to rest for 5–6 minutes. If it is too dry, add a tablespoon of water at a time until it is easy to form the mix into small balls. With your hands, make the arepa round and then flatten to about 4–5 inches in diameter.

Heat a lightly oiled cast iron skillet to medium heat. Put arepas to cook, about 5 minutes each side. They are done when you hear a hollow sound when you pat them. Remove from skillet and open each in the middle sideways. Fill with your favorite savory filling.

Makes 5–6 arepas.

The Venezuelan classics are contributed by Militza Garrillo, from Maracaibo, Venezuela. She traveled to the United States on vacation as a child with her parents, then chose to attend a U.S. college. Eventually, she became a restaurant entrepreneur in Venezuela then moved permanently to the United States in 2005. Today, she is a professor of English for speakers of other languages.

...

Cachapas

Courtesy of Militza Garrillo

1 cup of Sweet Corn mix—from the Harina P.A.N. company
1 cup of water
¼ cup milk
Oil or butter for the skillet

Mix the ingredients well in a bowl until all lumps are gone. Let it rest 5–6 minutes until the batter has thickened to a consistency that allows it to pour into a pan. Add more water or milk if not soft enough or add more corn mix as needed if it's too watery. It should be like a thick pancake batter.

Heat the skillet to medium, add enough oil or butter to grease it lightly. Using a ladle or measuring cup to pour, spread the mix to make a round disc. Cook for about 4–5 minutes each side until golden on both sides. Top with butter and cheese, or sausage, bacon, or pork as desired.

Makes 5–6.

Jamaicans

More than 300,000 Jamaicans are at home in South Florida, the largest community in the United States after New York. They are the largest immigrant group in Broward County, and Lauderhill is known as Jamaica Hill. South Florida is also referred to as Kingston 21. Jamaica's postal system is arranged in areas from 1–20; South Florida is lovingly added as 21. The island's largest charitable organization, Food for the Poor, has its corporate home in South Florida. Furthermore, the most popular Jamaican fruits and vegetables grow in the subtropical climate—including ackee, soursop, gungo peas, and yellow yam.

Jamaican Red Beans with Stew Beef by Joyce Facey

Courtesy of Nancy Hutton

1 lb. kidney beans, sorted and rinsed
1½ lbs. stew beef, trimmed of fat
Package of small, smoked ham hocks, trimmed
2 celery stalks, chopped
1 yellow onion, chopped
1 green pepper, chopped
3 garlic cloves, minced

Seasonings:
1 tsp. ground ginger
1 tsp. Nature's seasonings
1 tsp. Season-All Salt
1 Tbsp. black pepper
1 Tbsp. thyme
1 Tbsp. oregano
1 tsp. minced garlic
½ tsp. garlic powder
½ tsp. cayenne
¼ cup fine breadcrumbs
1 Tbsp. flour

Soak the beans in cold water for 4 hours, then drain water. Add new water to cover the beans in a pot and boil. Add the two meats to the beans. Then add the chopped vegetables.

Cover these with 3–5 cups of cold water. Bring to a boil and then lower the heat to a low simmer for 1½ hours. Then add the seasonings.

Simmer ½ hour to 1 hour; taste and correct seasonings as needed.

Add ¼ cup fine breadcrumbs and 1 tablespoon flour to thicken the sauce.

Geraldine Walker was born in St. Thomas, in Jamaica's Blue Mountain Valley region. She lived and taught for a decade in the Bahamas then moved to the United States in 1987. She is a retired professor of languages who continues to enjoy making dishes from many nations in her South Florida home.

...

Escoveitched Fish

Courtesy of Geraldine Walker

2 lb. fish, whole or fillets

Day 1:
Season fresh fish with a mix of lemon pepper seasoning and powdered jerk seasoning, according to taste. Cover and refrigerate.

Day 2:
Fry fish and make sauce.

Fry 2–5 whole garlic cloves until toasted brown in neutral oil in a skillet to infuse the oil with garlic flavor. Remove from oil, toss. Fry the fish in the garlic oil. When flesh is opaque, the fish is done. Put in a nonreactive container.

Make the sauce.

Escoveitch Sauce:
1 cup apple cider vinegar
1 cup water (varies, depending on taste for vinegar)
Pinch of salt
1 tsp. brown sugar
1 Scotch bonnet pepper or small piece of it
1½ cups of thin strips of various colored bell peppers
2–3 small yellow onions cut into thin rings
6 allspice seeds, whole
1 Tbsp. ketchup for coloring

Almost any type of fish can be used in this popular Jamaican recipe, served and welcomed at any meal. Snapper is a good choice.

In a saucepan, boil vinegar and water with a pinch of salt and brown sugar. Add pepper strips, onion rings, and allspice seeds. Let it return to a boil, then lower heat to simmer and cook for 5 minutes.

Pour over fried fish. Cover and refrigerate.

Day 3:
Heat fish in the microwave and serve with rice, ripe fried plantains, and a simple green salad.

Serves 6.

...

Green Plantain Puree

6 large, green, firm cooking bananas
Lemon juice
4 cups water
1/2 tsp. salt

Peel green bananas: scrape them to remove the fibrous strings, then rub them with lemon juice. Boil in salted water until tender. Drain and mash.

Serve in a mound on a hot dish to accompany meats. Serves 6.

...

Twice-Fried Green Plantains

Courtesy of Marisella Veiga

All green skins on the plantains—allow 1 plantain for 2 servings
Corn or vegetable oil for frying
Salt

Peel the plantain by cutting off ends and making 2 or 3 length-wise slits in it. Take care to not score the vegetable while making the slits. Pull the skin off.

Cut the plantain into 1 1/2- or 2-inch segments. Heat an inch of oil in a large skillet on medium. When oil is hot, place plantain segments in it. Turn sometimes. The first fry is done when the segments are golden; do not brown. Remove from skillet and place on brown grocery bag to drain and cool.

Then, using a piece of brown bag, stand the segment on an end and mash it to form a small disc. Around the edges, you will see some of it is not cooked. Repeat with each segment until all are ready for second fry.

Turn the skillet to medium high. Once the oil is evenly heated, return the *tostones* to the oil. Drain on paper towels, salt, and serve.

These are great appetizers too, alone or topped with samplings of creole-based dishes. In Puerto Rico I first saw them topped with caviar.

A salty, crunchy side dish with high-fiber content, the round, palm-sized, fried plantain slices called tostones are a challenge to French fries.

The Versatile Plantain

Most often called plantains, green or cooking bananas are a staple throughout the Caribbean and Latin America and in many U.S. homes and restaurants. Already popular in Africa at the time, the starchy, high-fiber plantain was brought to the New World from the Canary Islands in the late 1500s. Originally, they are thought to be from Southeast Asia. They can be mashed, fried, boiled, and/or baked, can be used as crusts, side dishes, or entrées, or made into desserts. They are found in various stages of ripeness in grocery stores throughout the state. They cannot be peeled by hand nor can they be eaten raw.

. . .

Plantain Chips

Courtesy of Marisella Veiga

All green-skinned plantains
Corn or vegetable oil for frying—as much as you'd use for French fries
Salt

Using a knife or mandolin, slice green plantains into thin, round chips or long strips called *tajadas* and fry in hot oil.

Remove from oil, drain on paper towels, salt, and serve.

...

Boiled Medium–Ripe Plantains

Courtesy of Marisella Veiga

Choose plantains that are yellow with some brown spots
1 plantain makes 2 sides
Water for boiling

Cut the ends off the plantain, cut it in half, then cut a slit down the middle of each. Do not remove skin. Place plantains in a pot of water, bring to boil, then lower to medium low.

A no-fat way to enjoy a plantain—it has much of the body of the green one along with some of the sweetness of the very ripe ones. It can be served at any meal.

Cook for 20 minutes. Test for doneness with a fork; if it goes through, the plantain is ready. Serve in skins as they are easy to remove.

...

Fried Ripe Plantains

Courtesy of Marisella Veiga

Cut the ends off the plantain and make a long slit to peel the skin. Then, slice it on a diagonal, each slice about 3/4 inch thick. Fry in medium hot oil, turning once.

Drain on paper towel and serve.

A well-ripened plantain is almost completely dark brown and feels soft when poked. A little yellow still appears on its skin.

...

Cuban Flan

(Caramel Custard)

1/4 cup sugar, divided
1 tsp. water
pinch of salt
2 cups milk
4 egg yolks, beaten
1/2 tsp. vanilla

In skillet, over very low heat, place 6 tablespoons sugar and the water and cook until sugar turns to golden syrup. Stir occasionally to prevent burning.

Pour into four custard cups and cool until firm. Beat together milk, beaten egg yolks, vanilla, and 2 tablespoons sugar until thoroughly blended. Pour over caramel in custard cups. Pour 1/2 inch boiling water in deep pan; place cups in water. Bake at 325°F about 1 hour 15 minutes, or until knife slipped into center comes out clean. Chill well. Invert onto chilled plates to serve. Serves 4.

Gold Coast Gourmet

...

Curried Egg Mold

2 envelopes unflavored gelatin
1 1/2 cup cold water
2 cups rich chicken stock, boiling
1 Tbsp. curry powder
1 1/2 cups mayonnaise
3 sliced hard-cooked eggs
6 sliced stuffed olives
1/2 cup finely sliced celery

Sprinkle gelatin on cold water until soft. Add gelatin mixture and curry powder to chicken stock. Stir to dissolve. Chill until slightly thick. Gradually stir in mayonnaise until blended. Mix in eggs, olives, and celery. Season to taste with salt and pepper. Turn into oiled 1 1/2-quart ring mold. Chill until firm; unmold on greens. If desired, garnish with greens, mayonnaise, and black olives. Serves 6–8.

...

Chicken Avocado Crepes

1/2 cup ripe olives, chopped
5 Tbsp. butter
5 Tbsp. flour
1 cup cream (or undiluted evaporated milk)

1 cup chicken broth
1/4 cup dry white wine
1 cup grated Swiss cheese
1/2 tsp. Worcestershire sauce
2 Tbsp. chopped parsley
Salt, pepper
2 cups diced cooked chicken
2 eggs
2 1/3 cup milk
1/2 cup sifted flour
1/2 tsp. salt
1 Tbsp. melted butter
1 large avocado, peeled and sliced
Paprika
Ripe olives for garnish

In large saucepan, melt 5 tablespoons butter and blend in 5 tablespoons flour. Pour in cream, broth, and wine. Cook, stirring constantly, until it boils and thickens. Stir in 1/4 cup cheese, Worcestershire sauce, parsley, and salt and pepper to taste; stir until smooth. Reserve 1 cup sauce; add olives and chicken to the rest.

To make crepes, beat eggs lightly; combine with milk. Sift 1/2 cup flour with 1/2 teaspoon salt. Combine with egg mixture; beat until smooth. Beat in melted butter. In lightly greased frying pan, pour 4 tablespoons batter; tilt pan to spread. Cook until golden brown, turning once. Repeat.

In greased baking dish, place crepes that have been filled with sauce, rolled, and secured with toothpick. Pour reserved sauce over crepes, sprinkle with remaining cheese and paprika. Bake in 375°F oven 15 minutes; then place under the broiler for a couple of minutes to brown. Top crepes with sliced avocado and whole ripe olives. Serves 6.

· · ·

JFK Salad Dressing

*Created by a Fontainebleau Hotel chef at
Miami Beach for John F. Kennedy*

5 whole eggs
1 clove garlic
1 tsp. salt

¼ tsp. pepper
2 Tbsp. paprika
1 tsp. prepared mustard
3 cups salad oil
1 cup olive oil
½ cup red wine vinegar

Crack eggs into bowl. Crush garlic and add. Combine with salt, pepper, paprika, and mustard; mix well. Add oils slowly, beating constantly. If mixture gets too thick, add a little vinegar. Continue beating, adding all of the vinegar until thoroughly blended. Correct salt and pepper to taste. Makes 6 cups.

. . .

Italian Meat Loaf

3 slices white bread
3 slices rye bread
1¼ cups beef stock
3 Tbsp. minced onion
1 Tbsp. prepared mustard
2 tsp. salt
½ tsp. parsley flakes
⅛ tsp. black pepper
¼ cup Parmesan cheese
2 eggs
2 lbs. ground beef
1 Tbsp. butter

Break bread into pieces in large mixing bowl. Add beef stock and onion. Let stand 10 minutes. With fork, mash bread pieces and beat mixture well. Add mustard, salt, parsley flakes, pepper, cheese, and eggs. Beat well with a fork. Add beef; mix thoroughly. Pack into oiled, 9 × 5 inch loaf pan. Dot top with butter. Bake in 375°F oven 60–70 minutes. Serves 8.

. . .

Ham–Cheese Fondue Soufflé

3 cups French or Italian bread, cubed
3 cups cooked ham, cubed
½ lb. cheddar cheese, in 1-inch cubes

3 Tbsp. flour
1 Tbsp. dry mustard
3 Tbsp. butter, melted
4 eggs
3 cups milk
Few drops red hot sauce

Butter an 8-cup, straight-sided casserole dish. In bottom, place a layer of cubed bread, then a layer of ham, then a layer of cubed cheese. Mix flour with mustard, sprinkle over cheese. Drizzle butter or margarine over top. Beat eggs; add milk and red hot sauce; pour over layers in casserole dish. Cover; chill at least 4 hours, preferably overnight. (The secret of this dish is the long chilling.) Bake uncovered in 350°F oven 1 hour. Serve at once. Serves 6.

Jewish Specialties

...

Sauerbraten with Potato Pancakes

3 lb. round steak
1 pint cider vinegar water
3 bay leaves
3 peppercorns
2 Tbsp. flour
Salt, pepper, paprika
1 tsp. allspice
1 Tbsp. cooking oil
6 carrots
6 onions, sliced
12 gingersnaps
1 Tbsp. sugar

Place meat in bowl, pour over vinegar and enough water to cover. Add bay leaves and peppercorns. Refrigerate 3 days. Combine flour, salt, pepper, paprika, and allspice. Drain meat; shake in bag filled with flour mixture. Brown meat lightly in hot oil. Place meat in heavy saucepan with sliced carrots, onions, and 2 cups of vinegar marinade. Cover and simmer 2 hours. Crumble gingersnaps; add gingersnaps and sugar to liquid around meat. Add salt and pepper to taste. Serve with potato pancakes. Serves 6.

· · ·

Potato Pancakes (Latkes)

2 cups potatoes
2 eggs, well beaten
1 Tbsp. flour or matzo meal
Vegetable oil
Pinch baking powder
1 Tbsp. grated onion
Salt, pepper to taste

Peel and grate potatoes. Thoroughly combine all ingredients. Drop by tablespoonfuls into hot oil in frying pan. Fry until crisp at edges on under side; turn and fry until done. Serves 4.

· · ·

Passover Jelly Roll

1/2 cup sifted matzo cake meal
1/2 cup potato flour
6 eggs, separated
1 cup sugar
Juice and rind of 1/2 lemon
1 Tbsp. cold water
1/4 tsp. salt
1 cup raspberry preserves
Confectioners' sugar

Line a 10 × 15 inch jelly roll pan with wax paper. Sift together matzo cake meal and potato flour. Beat egg yolks with sugar until thick and lemon colored. Stir in lemon juice, grated rind, and water. Gradually add sifted dry ingredients, stirring to make a thick batter. Beat egg whites and salt until stiff but not dry. Fold gently into batter.

Turn batter into jelly roll pan. Bake in 325°F oven about 20 minutes or until just done. Don't let edges brown and harden. Remove from oven, peel off paper. Turn onto a towel that has been spread with sugar. Trim off crisp edges. Roll cake in towel; cool completely. Unroll. Remove towel. Spread with preserves. Roll again, dust lightly with confectioner's sugar. Serves 10.

Sephardic or Spanish Jews—
Expulsion and Dispersal

Ferdinand II of Aragon and Isabella of Castile's marriage in 1469 was designed to unify Spain. By 1478, the monarchs introduced a brutal policy of homogenization, the Inquisition. On July 30, 1492, Spain's entire Jewish community, some 200,000 people, was expelled. Meanwhile, Italian explorer Christopher Columbus received financial support from the monarchs for a voyage to find new lands. He sailed with many crypto-Jews or *conversos*. These events marked the beginning of the dispersal of Sephardic Jews. Many settled in Puerto Rico. Yet the Inquisition reached into New World colonies. Many Sephardic Jews moved into the island's mountainous interior, as Costa Mauri's ancestors did, eventually intermarrying. Her grandparents moved and settled in Philadelphia about 1920. They were fully bilingual when they arrived as a result of the United States running the schools on the island after the Spanish-American War. Since medieval times, the foundational sauté known today as "sofrito" has been in Catalonian kitchens. Sephardic Jews incorporated it into their dishes, especially since meats cooked in sofrito kept well over the Sabbath, when work was prohibited.

· · ·

Stewed Chicken Sofrito

Courtesy of Mona Costa Mauri

3 lbs. chicken breasts, skin on, bone in
1/3 cup olive oil
8 small yellow onions peeled
10 whole garlic cloves, peeled and minced
3/4 cup chicken broth plus more if needed
1 tsp. paprika
1 tsp. turmeric
1/2 tsp. curry powder
1/2 tsp. ground white pepper
1/2 tsp. allspice

Salt and freshly ground black pepper
8 yellow potatoes, cut into even wedges
Olive oil for frying

Preheat oven to 300°F. Heat 4 tablespoons of oil in a frying pan and brown the meat on all sides. Generously grease a wide, flat baking pan (use 5 tablespoons of oil) and place the meat, onions, and garlic.

Mix the broth with the spices, bring to a simmer and pour over the chicken. Test and adjust the seasoning. If more broth is needed, add now. Cover the pan with foil and cook for an hour in the oven. Shake the pan once or twice during the time it is cooking. Once done, the dish can be refrigerated and stored there.

When getting ready to serve, heat oil for frying the potatoes in a skillet and fry until golden brown. Transfer to paper towels to drain. You may roast them in a 400°F oven if preferred.

Put chicken and onions on a platter and add the potatoes around the plate. Add and mix in two cups chopped parsley. Lemon wedges should accompany this dish.

Tropical Fruit Specialties

. . .

Caracas Pineapple Coupe

2 fresh pineapples
1 cantaloupe
1/4 cup maraschino cordial
1/4 cup Cointreau cordial
1 pint orange sherbet
1 pint lime sherbet
1/4 cup shredded coconut
1/2 pint heavy cream, whipped

Cut pineapples in half lengthwise; scoop out center, leaving 1/2-inch border of fruit around edge. Dice scooped-out pineapple. Cut cantaloupe, clean, and cut fruit into balls or cubes. Combine the two cordials, pineapple chunks, and cantaloupe balls; refrigerate for 4 hours. Fill pineapple shells with fruit. Top with orange and lime sherbets, sprinkle

with shredded coconut, and circle with whipped cream. Serves 4
generously.

...

Mango Frost

1 heaping cup sliced mangoes
2 Tbsp. powdered milk
Juice of 1 lime
1 Tbsp. sugar
1 Tbsp. light rum
Crushed ice

Combine first 5 ingredients in blender. Add crushed ice to fill container.
Blend at high speed until mixture thickens to the consistency of soft
sherbet. Serve immediately topped with a sprig of mint, with a spoon or
straw, depending on thickness. Serves 2.

*Deceptively simple, this recipe is an all-time favorite. Especially good after
a heavy meal, it has marvelous tropical flavor and a texture like soft sherbet.
Peaches may be substituted for the mangoes, if you like.*

...

Lime French Dressing

5 Tbsp. salad oil
$1/2$ tsp. salt
$1/2$ tsp. paprika
$1/2$ tsp. prepared mustard
1 Tbsp. lime juice
1 tsp. onion juice
$1/2$ tsp. garlic salt

Place all ingredients in small bottle; cover tightly and shake well. Chill.
Process in blender just before serving. Makes $1/4$ cup of tart dressing—
perfect with greens, avocados, or vegetable combinations.

...

Lime Dessert Sauce

1 Tbsp. cornstarch
1/2 cup sugar
Cold water
1/4 cup boiling water
2 Tbsp. butter or margarine
2 1/2 Tbsp. lime juice

Mix cornstarch with sugar. Blend to smooth paste with a little cold water. Gradually stir paste into boiling water. Continue stirring over moderate heat until thickened. Remove from stove. Add butter and lime juice. This tangy, sweet sauce is delicious hot or cold, over pudding or fritters. Makes about 1 1/2 cups.

...

Florida Green Ice Cream

1 medium avocado, de-seeded and mashed (3/4 cup of pulp)
2/3 cup sugar
1/2 tsp. salt
3 1/2 Tbsp. lime juice
1 cup pineapple juice
1 1/2 cups light cream

Combine all ingredients and stir until thoroughly blended. Freeze in ice cube tray until almost firm. Break up and whip until light and fluffy. Turn into fancy one-quart mold and refreeze 2 hours or until firm. Serves 6.

...

Cream of Avocado Soup

1 quart thin white sauce
1 cup avocado pulp, finely mashed
1/6 tsp. ginger
Pinch of salt
Grated rind of 1 orange
6 Tbsp. heavy cream, whipped
Paprika
12 thin slices of avocado

Combine white sauce, avocado, ginger, salt, and orange rind. Beat until well blended. Heat but do not boil. Ladle soup into 6 individual serving bowls. Garnish with dollop of whipped cream, dash of paprika, and thin slices of avocado. Serves 6.

. . .

Prize-Winning Shrimp-Stuffed Avocados

3 large avocados
3 Tbsp. lime juice
1 tsp. salt, divided
4 Tbsp. butter
6 Tbsp. flour
1/8 tsp. black pepper
1 1/2 cups milk
1/2 cup sliced, cooked celery
1/4 cup pimiento, minced
1 cup boiled shrimp
2/3 cup grated cheddar cheese

Cut avocados in half lengthwise; peel, and remove pit. Sprinkle with lime juice and 1/2 teaspoon salt. Melt butter, blend in flour, add remaining salt, pepper, and milk; cook until thickened, stirring constantly. Add celery, pimiento, and shrimp. Fill avocados with shrimp mixture; cover with grated cheese, place in baking pan. Pour boiling water in pan to a depth of 1/2 inch and bake in 350°F oven 15 minutes. Serves 6.

. . .

Kumquat (or Calamondin) Marmalade

1 quart kumquats, halved and seeded
1 cup sugar per cup of fruit
Juice of 1/2 lemon

Place halved, seeded fruit in enough water to cover it; cook until skin is soft. Leave fruit in pan, cover, and let soak in juices overnight. Measure 1 cup sugar to each cup of fruit. Add juice of half a lemon (or whole lemon for added tartness). Cook over very high heat until it boils, then start stirring and cook, stirring constantly, 15 minutes—but never more than

20 minutes! This makes a marmalade of soft consistency. Pour into jars and seal.

. . .

Surinam Cherry Jam

3 1/4 cups sugar
2 cups water
3 1/4 cups Surinam cherries, seeded

Combine sugar and water, bring to boil, and add cherries. Boil cherries in syrup 20–25 minutes, or until juice thickens slightly but does not gel. Pour into hot jars and seal.

. . .

Bananas Flambe

3 Tbsp. butter
2 Tbsp. brown sugar
1/4 cup banana liqueur
1/4 cup light rum
2 bananas, peeled, sliced lengthwise
2 Tbsp. brandy

Melt butter in chafing dish or frying pan. Add brown sugar and cook until bubbling and syrupy. Put in sliced bananas, roll in sauce, and spoon sauce over until glazed. Push bananas to one side; heat other side of pan until it is dry. Pour in banana liqueur; ignite. Spoon flaming liqueur over fruit until flames die. Repeat with rum, then brandy, each time letting flames die. Serve over vanilla ice cream. Serves 3.

. . .

Guava Cheese Pie

1/2 cup guava paste
1/2 cup cream
3 eggs
1 lb. sieved cottage cheese
1 Tbsp. lime juice
Pinch of salt

8-inch graham cracker crumb crust
Dash of mace

Chop guava paste into small cubes. Heat in cream over lowest possible heat until paste partially melts but tiny blobs of paste remain. Beat eggs well until fluffy and lemon colored. Add to cheese together with guava mixture, lime juice, and salt. Pour into crumb crust; sprinkle with mace. Bake in 350°F oven 45–55 minutes. Makes one 8-inch pie.

. . .

Papaya Sundae

1/4 cup honey
1/4 cup cream
1/2 cup sugar
1 Tbsp. butter or margarine
1/4 cup lime or lemon juice
1/2 cup sweetened, flaked coconut
1 papaya
1 quart vanilla ice cream
Garnishes: mint sprigs, stemmed cherries

Combine honey, cream, sugar, and butter. Boil 3 minutes, stirring constantly. Chill. Stir in lime juice and coconut. Halve papaya; scoop out seeds and membrane. Peel; cut crosswise into 1/2-inch slices. Scoop ice cream into sundae dishes and encircle it with papaya slices. Pour sauce on top, or serve it at the table.

Garnish with mint and cherries. Serves 6.

. . .

Mango Chutney, Indian Style

4 lbs. green mangoes
2 quarts vinegar
2 lbs. sugar
2 Tbsp. white mustard seed
1 Tbsp. ground dried chili pepper
4 tsp. allspice
2 cups dark raisins
1 clove garlic
1 lb. preserved ginger in syrup

Peel and cut fruit; add 1 quart vinegar. Boil 20 minutes. Combine sugar and second quart of vinegar and boil until thick syrup forms, about 1 hour. Pour off most of the liquid from fruit and add to this syrup. Boil this combination until thickened, about 15 minutes. Combine this thick syrup with the rest of the ingredients and fruit except ginger; cook 30 minutes. Add chopped ginger and its syrup; cook 10 minutes longer. Remove garlic. Pour into sterilized jars and seal. To improve flavor, let stand in the sun for three days. Makes about 4 quarts.

Freezing Mangoes

Use high-quality mangoes at peak of ripeness. Peel and cut from seed in slices. Pack into moisture-vapor-proof containers, packing down to eliminate air spaces. Leave 1/4 inch of space at top. Pour sweetened limeade over to cover. (This prevents fruit from drying out and losing texture and flavor.) Seal and freeze, placing against walls of home freezer.

. . .

Pineapple Cheese Dip

8 oz. whipped cream cheese
2 cups shredded cheddar cheese
1/4 cup milk
3 Tbsp. white Port wine (or grape juice)
1 tsp. Worcestershire sauce
1/2 tsp. salt
1 ripe sweet pineapple
1/2 tsp. dry mustard

The tropical taste of pineapple flavors a tangy cheese dip.

Beat together cheeses, milk, wine, Worcestershire sauce, salt, and dry mustard in bowl. Cut pineapple in half crosswise and cut pineapple meat out of bottom half to make a shell; cut fruit into cubes. Fill shell with cheese mixture. Refrigerate until ready to serve. Cut crown off top half of pineapple, cut off rind, cut into quarters, cut away core, and cut into chunks.

Refrigerate. Let cheese-stuffed pineapple stand at room temperature for 15 minutes to soften before serving. Place on serving plate and surround with pineapple chunks. Spear pineapple chunks with cocktail picks and dip into cheese mixture. Makes about 2½ cups cheese dip.

• • •

Val Mayfield's Tropical Fruit Pie

Crust:
1 cups almond macaroon crumbs
¼ cup confectioners' sugar
½ cup melted butter or margarine

Filling:
1 cup crushed pineapple
2 Tbsp. flour
5 Tbsp. sugar, divided
1½ cups fresh or frozen coconut
½ tsp. coconut flavoring
2 large bananas, peeled and brushed with lemon juice
1 cup heavy cream, whipped
Maraschino cherries

In medium bowl, toss macaroon crumbs, confectioners' sugar, and butter with fork until well mixed. Press mixture into bottom and sides of 8-inch pie plate. Refrigerate.

Combine pineapple, flour, and 3 tablespoons sugar in saucepan and cook over medium heat until thickened, stirring constantly, about 10 minutes. Cool.

How to Open a Coconut

To open fresh coconut, first make a hole in the eye and drain out the milk. Place nut in 350°F oven 20 minutes. Remove; let cool. Wrap coconut in a towel and crack it with a hammer—one easy pull and the meat is out. Peel the brown skin away from the meat. Refrigerate unused coconut and milk.

Open coconut, remove the meat, and grate it. Mix grated coconut with 2 tablespoons sugar and flavoring. Toast 1/2 cup of sweetened, flavored coconut lightly in 250°F oven; set the rest aside.

Slice the bananas and arrange them in the bottom of the pie crust. Spread cooled pineapple mixture over bananas. Cover with 1 cup untoasted coconut. Top with whipped cream. Sprinkle with 1/2 cup toasted coconut.

Refrigerate. Just before serving, garnish with maraschino cherries. Makes one 8-inch pie.

Homestead and the Colorful Florida Keys

Pigeon Key lies in the shadow of the Overseas Highway, which travels more than 100 miles out in the Gulf to reach Key West.

Take U.S. 1 toward the Keys, but make sure you spend some time in the Homestead and surrounding areas before leaving the mainland. South Miami-Dade County has been and continues to be a major agricultural area that provides subtropical and tropical fruits and vegetables during the winter months. Many Midwestern farmers and their families were early settlers.

The Redland or Redlands—either are acceptable—is named for the potholes or pockets of red clay covering the limestone beds. It refers to the entire agricultural area stretching northwest from Florida City, Homestead, and the U.S. 1 and Krome Avenue corridors. U-picks and nurseries dot the area. Avocado groves occupy 8,000 acres. Potato farming was once king, but in the early 2000s, the last fields were harvested.

The city of Homestead lies between two national parks: the Everglades National Park to the west and south and Biscayne National Park to the east. In 1992 Hurricane Andrew destroyed homes, businesses, churches, nurseries, migrant labor camps, and schools. The Homestead Air Force Base was decimated. Full recovery came and now, more growth continues. Florida City is a home for a State Farmers Market.

Knaus Berry Farms is noteworthy. It is said there are two seasons in South Miami-Dade County: when Knaus Berry Farms is open and when it is closed. At times, more than 100 people wait in line for their famous cinnamon rolls, strawberries, and strawberry milkshakes.

Two brothers—Jess and Harley Knaus—moved from Missouri to South Dade County and bought 80 acres of land in 1924. By 1954, two of Jess' sons, Ray and Russell, started raising strawberries. The family business continues.

The Moehlings, who were farmers, moved to South Dade County from Illinois in 1953, with three-month-old Robert. At age six, he began selling leftover produce at a crossroads. It became Florida's most famous fruit stand: the Robert Is Here Fruit Stand. Today, you'll find him selling rare and exotic fruits and vegetables as well as incredible smoothies and milkshakes and juices, including *guarapo*, sugar cane juice. All ages will enjoy spending time there.

The Preston B. Bird and Mary Heinlein Fruit and Spice Park is a 37-acre subtropical and tropical botanical garden with more than 500 varieties of fruit, herbs, spices, and nuts. For example, it has more than 180 varieties of mango and 15 varieties of jackfruit. The park is dedicated to educating people about the bounty surrounding them, offering tours, classes, and events.

A driving force behind the public park's creation, Mary Heinlein was from a South Dade pioneer family. Her parents moved to the area from Kansas and became homesteaders in 1910, one of the few lasting early settlers. As a child, she helped grow tomatoes and peanuts. The park is the only one of its kind in the United States.

Schnebly Redland's Winery & Brewery celebrates the area's abundant tropical fruit—mango, guava, lychee, and passion fruit, to name a few. Grapes are excluded. Their restaurant makes use of locally sourced foods as well.

. . .

German Potato Salad

Courtesy of Holly Krummenacher Iglesias

10 small red or white potatoes
1/2 pound bacon
1 Tbsp. flour
1 cup vinegar
1 tsp. salt
1/2 tsp. sugar
1/8 tsp. pepper
1 medium onion, finely chopped
1 cup chopped celery
3 hard-boiled eggs, sliced

Boil potatoes until tender. As potatoes cook, fry bacon until crisp, drain on paper towels, then chop. Peel warm potatoes and slice. Stir flour into the bacon drippings in the skillet until smooth. Add vinegar, salt, sugar, and pepper. Stir until slightly thickened. Toss in the potatoes, bacon, onion, and celery. Serve warm, garnished with egg slices.

Serves 10–12.

. . .

Sour Cream Coffee Cake

Courtesy of Holly Krummenacher Iglesias

Cake batter:
1 cup butter
1 cup sugar

3 eggs

1 tsp. vanilla

2 1/2 cups sifted flour

2 tsp. baking powder

1 tsp. baking soda

1/2 tsp. salt

1 cup sour cream

Topping:

3/4 cup brown sugar

1/2 cup chopped pecans, walnuts, or almonds

2 tsp. cinnamon

Cream butter and sugar. Mix in eggs and vanilla. (Mixture will appear curdled.) Add dry ingredients alternately with sour cream. Pour half of batter into greased 13 × 9 inch pan or two 8-inch square pans. Mix ingredients for topping. Sprinkle a third of the topping over the batter. Top with rest of batter, then rest of topping. Bake at 375°F about 30 minutes for 13 × 9 inch pan, 45 minutes for square pans. Serves 8–12.

Regina Krummenacher made sure her daughter left home prepared for young adult life in college and then as a newly married person by giving her two cookbooks: The Joy of Cooking as well as another published by the mothers of her Catholic high school in St. Louis. These two cookbooks were carried along to various homes. Today, they sit on her South Florida bookshelf alongside Cocina Criolla by Cuba's Nitza Villapol.

. . .

Ev's Tuna Fish Salad

Courtesy of Nancy Swanson Wilson

3 cans of tuna, chunk light in water preferred

Mayonnaise, enough to hold it together

1/2 of a large apple, diced

1–2 stalks of celery, diced

1/4 cup yellow onion, diced

3 heaping Tbsp. sweet relish

Mix ingredients in proportions you prefer. Serve immediately or refrigerate.

. . .

Basil Roasted Vegetables

Courtesy of Marisella Veiga

1/2 cup fresh basil, chopped
2 Tbsp. fresh Cuban or Greek oregano, chopped
4 Tbsp. olive oil
3 Tbsp. balsamic vinegar
1/2 tsp. salt
3 garlic cloves, minced
2 medium zucchinis, chunks
1 medium red pepper, chunked
2 yellow crookneck squash, chunked
1 large red onion, wedged
8–12 mushrooms

Preheat oven to 425°F. Combine basil, oregano, oil, vinegar, salt, and garlic in a large bowl. Add vegetables and toss to coat. Arrange them in a shallow roasting pan and bake for 35 to 45 minutes, stirring once to ensure more even roasting.

Serves 6.

. . .

Cuban Avocado and Pineapple Salad

Courtesy of Marisella Veiga

1 Florida avocado, cut in chunks
2 cups fresh pineapple, chunked
1 small yellow onion, chopped
Olive oil
1–2 limes
Salt and pepper to taste

Ingredients should be at room temperature. Mix vegetables in a serving bowl, add fresh lime juice and olive oil, then salt and pepper, toss and serve.

No romantic novel could have a plot more exciting than the real-life history of the Florida Keys, a chain of white coral islands strung in a half moon from the mainland to Key West. Like a hair-raising adventure tale, it bristles with violence and sudden death, alternating with times of peace and prosperity.

Early Spanish adventurers exploring to the southernmost island found piles of human bones, presumably men slain during a battle with the fierce Calusas. They named the place *Cayo Hueso*—Bone Key in Spanish— which was corrupted to "Key West."

In 1513, Ponce de León sailed past the rocky islands and gave them a highly appropriate name, Los Martires, because they looked like suffering people.

Ponce de León claimed Florida for Spain when he came searching for gold and the Fountain of Youth. In 1521 he sailed to a place near Charlotte Harbor, where he intended to settle a colony but was wounded in the thigh by a Calusa poisoned arrow. He died in Havana, Cuba. Spanish efforts were followed again by Hernanado de Soto's expedition in 1539. This expedition is credited with launching our state's livestock industry, as it brought cattle and swine, all free-range. Eventually, the king of Spain abandoned the idea of settling Florida and moved his ships to Mexico and South America to loot them of gold, silver, jewels, and precious woods.

Twice a year, these treasure-laden ships passed through the Bahama Channel and the treacherous, reef-bound water along the Keys, and brought the Keys their most despicable residents—cutthroat English pirates and French buccaneers who preyed on stricken ships and attacked unwary ones.

Even with the building of a new Overseas Highway, prosperity did not return until World War II. By 1990, Key West had a population of about 24,800.

Life on the Keys bred a special kind of men and women—hardy people with valor and the toughness of pioneers. A strong Cockney accent identifies many of them with the Englishmen who first left the Bahamas for the Keys to cut scarce wood and find turtles. Proudly they call themselves "Conchs" after the rose-pink mollusk that once was a staple in the Keys diet. In 1982, their pioneering spirit rose to form a movement for an independent Conch Republic. Some citizens advocated for secession from the United States as a result of its border patrol policies at the start of the Overseas Highway.

The Conchs built humble but sturdy dwellings on the white coral islands that seem to float on the blue-green sea. And they survived on food from the sea, canned foods brought in by boat, coconuts, precious garden vegetables, and fruit from the hardy little Key lime trees. Life was lonely and secluded, but they loved it.

Because there was no refrigeration, canned condensed milk was in great demand. With it, the Conchs produced a true masterpiece, Key lime pie.

Their fish was plentiful: crawfish (Florida spiny lobster), stone crabs, grunt, snapper, grouper, sea trout, bonefish, mackerel, kingfish, and pink jumbo shrimp. Great green sea turtles weighing up to 300 pounds were a major food source. Today, all sea turtles are protected species, and so is the Queen Conch that gave the Keys pioneers their nickname.

Conch foods are a fascinating blend of Southern Cracker cooking, zesty Latin, and spicy Caribbean. Conch seafood is a world away from simple New England dishes—but it is spectacularly good.

Woven into the cuisine are tropical foods such as avocado, plantain, carissa, kumquat, guava, papaya, pineapple, and coconut. Many of these meld with seafood into unforgettable salads. Yet the most memorable dish is, of course, Key lime pie. Just be sure when you try it on the Keys to ask for the original recipe made with sweetened condensed milk. Conchs consider this the *only* one, and variations as outrageous imitations.

No trip to Key West would be complete without observing an old tradition: visiting Mallory Square at sunset when street vendors sell banana bread, as musicians, bicycle riders, and artists gather on the dock to salute the sun as it sinks into the ocean in crimson and golden splendor. In 1984, Mallory Square pier opened to cruise ships, which increased tourism but altered the original, more intimate setting. Still, the spirit of celebration at day's end continues. No matter where we live, community life would be greatly improved if we celebrated both sunrise and sunset together daily.

The tropical beauty and unexcelled fishing of Key West have lured many celebrities including the late President Truman. Literary greats like Ernest Hemingway and Tennessee Williams made their homes in Key West. Other writers, such as Shel Silverstein, Robert Frost, Elizabeth Bishop, and Judy Blume have, too. Visitors jam the old city to see the picturesque cedar and hardwood homes built by seafaring men, to attend Wreckers' Balls and other events during fun-filled old Island Days in mid-winter.

In 1979, several business owners created a costumed parade called Fantasy Fest. It has grown to a 10-day annual festival with more than 60 parties along with a parade, drawing more than 75,000 people.

In spite of the changes, somehow, Key West has retained its quaint charm—a tropical oasis unlike any other.

Keys Seafood Recipes

. . .

Crawfish Chelow

(Florida Lobster)
Eat this in soup bowls with Tender-Crust Cuban Bread (page 91)

2 medium onions, chopped
6 cloves garlic, finely chopped
1 large green pepper, chopped
$1/4 - 1/3$ cup olive oil
2 8-oz. cans tomato sauce
1 6-oz. can tomato paste
1 tsp. salt
$1/8$ tsp. pepper
3 bay leaves
$1/4$ tsp. oregano
4 large or 6 small crawfish

Fry onions, garlic, and green pepper in oil until tender but not browned, stirring occasionally. Use enough oil to prevent scorching. Add tomato sauce and tomato paste. Rinse each can with a tablespoon or two of water and add this water to the stew. Add salt, pepper, bay leaves, and oregano. Remove crawfish from shells, chop in small pieces, and add. Cook, uncovered, about 20 minutes, until slightly cooked down. Serve hot in soup bowls. Serves 6.

···

Minced Crawfish

1/2 large green pepper, chopped
1/2 large onion, chopped
6 small cloves garlic, finely chopped
3 Tbsp. oil, bacon drippings, or shortening
2 bay leaves
4 large or 6 small crawfish
1 8-oz. can tomato sauce
1/4 tsp. oregano
1 1/2 tsp. Worcestershire sauce
1 tsp. salt
1/8 tsp. pepper

Fry green pepper, onion, and garlic in oil until tender but not browned, stirring now and then. Use more oil, if needed, to prevent scorching. Remove crawfish from shells and cut fine. Add to onion mixture with bay leaves and stir. Cook until very hot, about 3 minutes. Add tomato sauce and a little water to rinse can. Add oregano, Worcestershire sauce, salt, and pepper. Cook uncovered about 15 minutes, until some of the liquid has cooked out. Minced crawfish should be moist, but not runny with juice. Serve over hot, fluffy rice. Serves 8.

Minced crawfish is similar to the chelow but less soupy. It is served over white rice and accompanied by black beans, green salad, and Cuban bread.

···

Conch Chowder

1/4 lb. salt pork
2 medium onions, chopped
4 cloves garlic, crushed
1 large green pepper, chopped
1 16-oz. can tomatoes
1 6-oz. can tomato paste
2 quarts hot water
1 tsp. poultry seasoning
8 large conchs
1 Tbsp. vinegar

1 tsp. salt
1/2 tsp. pepper
1 Tbsp. oregano
4 bay leaves
2 Tbsp. barbecue sauce
9 medium potatoes, peeled and sliced

Dice salt pork and fry in large pot. Add onions, garlic, and green pepper. Cook until tender but not browned. Add tomatoes, tomato paste, hot water, and poultry seasoning; cook over low heat while preparing conch.

Pound conchs with back of knife to break up tough tissue. Chop. Add to chowder. Bring to a boil. Add vinegar, salt, pepper, oregano, bay leaves, and barbecue sauce. Cover and bring to a boil, then turn heat low and simmer 2 hours. Add potatoes and simmer until potatoes are tender, about 20 minutes. Serves 8 generously.

Queen Conchs may not be taken from Florida waters but may be purchased at some seafood markets. They are imported from the Caribbean where they are raised commercially.

. . .

Dolphin Amandine

The fish that is usually called "dolphin" here is often sold under its Hawaiian name of "mahi-mahi." It is not the big, playful mammal that performs at Sea World.

12 1/2-inch-thick dolphin fillets (about 6 oz. each)
1 Tbsp. cooking oil
1 tsp. salt
1/8 tsp. white pepper
1–1 1/2 tsp. paprika
1/2 cup (1 stick) butter
1 6-oz. package slivered almonds

Place dolphin fillets in a lightly oiled shallow pan. No rack is needed. Sprinkle with salt, pepper, and paprika. Cook 1 minute in center of electric oven, then 6–7 minutes close under broiler. If using a gas oven, cook 1 minute in upper part of oven, 6–7 minutes under broiler flame.

Meanwhile, melt butter. Add almonds and cook over very low heat about 5 minutes, until pale brown. Pour over hot dolphin and serve at once. Serves 12.

Baked Mackerel in Spanish Sauce

Key West families of Spanish origin use fresh garlic freely, as seen in the sauce, which must be done for authentic flavor. You may, of course, reduce it to suit your taste.

1 3-lb. King or Spanish mackerel
Cooking oil
Salt and pepper
1/2 cup tomato juice
1 Tbsp. onion, finely chopped
1 cup Spanish Sauce
1/4 cup bread crumbs
2 Tbsp. butter

Clean fish, rub with cooking oil, and season with salt and pepper. Place fish in oiled pan; pour on tomato juice, then sprinkle with onion. Bake at 350°F about 30 minutes, basting occasionally. Remove from oven; pour Spanish Sauce over fish, sprinkle top with bread crumbs, and dot with butter. Place in oven until browned. Serves 6.

Spanish Sauce:
2 green peppers, coarsely chopped
5 cloves garlic, finely chopped
1/2 cup fresh, light olive oil
Onions, coarsely chopped
1 28-oz. can tomatoes
1 10 1/2-oz. can tomato puree
Bay leaves
1/4 tsp. oregano
1 1/2 tsp. Worcestershire sauce
Juice of 1 lime
Salt and pepper

In saucepan, heat olive oil and cook garlic and green peppers until latter are almost tender. Add onion; cook until tender but not browned. Stir in tomatoes, tomato puree, bay leaves, oregano, Worcestershire sauce, lime juice, and salt and pepper to taste. Simmer until well blended, about 20 minutes, stirring occasionally. Makes about 2 1/2 cups sauce.

Ocean Reef Grouper Chowder

1 fresh grouper, about 5 lbs.
1 gallon water
1 Tbsp. salt
1 large onion, coarsely chopped
4 whole cloves
1 bay leaf
1 large stalk celery, chopped
1 stick butter
1 medium onion, finely chopped
1 tsp. curry powder
1/2 tsp. rosemary
1/2 tsp. oregano
1/2 tsp. leaf thyme
1 1/2 cups flour
2 tsp. monosodium glutamate
About 1 quart light cream

Clean grouper and cut off head. Place grouper with head in large kettle with water, salt, large onion, cloves, bay leaf, and celery. Bring to a boil; reduce heat to simmer, and cook about 12 minutes, or until fish flakes when pierced with a fork. Take pot off the heat; strain liquid. Remove fish from bones and cut in bite-size pieces. Sauté onion in butter in a saucepan until tender but not brown. Add curry powder, rosemary, oregano, thyme, and flour, stirring until smooth. Stir in stock drained from grouper, and monosodium glutamate. Stir until smooth, then reduce to simmer and cook 20–25 minutes.

Using 1/3 as much cream as fish liquid, bring cream to boil in a separate pan. Pour cream into chowder; add grouper chunks. Reheat; serve at once. Makes 20 servings—enough for a chowder party. (Tip: Freeze leftover chowder and reheat, but do not boil.)

···
Pompano Stew

¹/₂ lb. salt pork
4 medium onions, chopped
3 tomatoes, peeled and chopped
1 clove garlic
1 small green pepper, chopped
1 cup celery, chopped
4 medium potatoes
1¹/₂ quarts water
3 lb. pompano, cut in steaks
1 tsp. salt
¹/₈ tsp. pepper
2 Tbsp. flour

Dice salt pork and fry. Add onions, tomatoes, garlic, green pepper, and celery. Cook until tender, stirring occasionally. Add potatoes and water. Cover: cook until potatoes are tender, about 20 minutes. Add pompano, salt, and pepper, and cook until tender, 10–15 minutes. Stir flour into a little water to make a smooth paste; stir into broth, cooking and stirring until thick and smooth. Serves 5–6.

···
Key West Paella

¹/₂ cup olive oil
4 cloves garlic
2 bay leaves
1 tsp. oregano
2 lbs. chicken pieces
¹/₂ lb. diced pork loin
1 cup chopped onion
1 chorizo (Spanish sausage)
¹/₂ cup diced cooked ham
4 raw oysters
4 raw clams
8 raw shrimp, peeled and deveined
1 cup long grain rice
4 cups hot stock or water
1¹/₂ tsp. salt

¹/₄ tsp. pepper
1 tsp. monosodium glutamate
¹/₄ tsp. powdered saffron
1 large green pepper, sliced
2–3 pimientos, halved
1 8-oz. can peas, drained
Optional garnishes: hard-cooked eggs, asparagus

Heat olive oil in paella (large ovenproof casserole); sauté garlic and bay leaves gently 3 minutes; remove. Add oregano, chicken, and pork to oil and cook, turning until browned and almost done. Add onion, sausage (cut in inch-long pieces), and ham. Sauté 3 minutes. Add oysters, clams, shrimp, rice, stock, salt, pepper, monosodium glutamate, and saffron. (To use thread saffron, crush and heat in a spoonful of water held over the pot for a minute or two, then add.) Boil for 10 minutes. Arrange green pepper, pimientos, and peas on top for decoration. Cover and bake in 375°F oven for 15 minutes. Serves 6-8.

. . .

Shrimp Cocktail

1 lb. large shrimp
1 quart water
1 Tbsp. salt
1 Tbsp. vinegar
Lettuce leaves
Cocktail sauce

Tip: Beware of overcooking. It makes shrimp tough.

Wash shrimp in shells under cold running water. Drop into COLD water, allowing 1 tablespoon salt for each quart of water. When water boils, add a tablespoon of vinegar. Time cooking from the moment boiling starts, and boil shrimp just 2 minutes, no longer. Drain and remove shells; devein. Chill. Line cocktail glasses with lettuce, fill with shrimp, and serve with Cocktail Sauce.

Serves 4.

Cocktail Sauce:
¹/₂ cup tomato ketchup
6 Tbsp. lemon or lime juice
¹/₈ tsp. salt
1 Tbsp. grated horseradish

3 drops Tabasco sauce

1/2 tsp. celery salt

Blend all ingredients, chill in refrigerator.

. . .

Sloppy Joe

Courtesy of Sara Menendez

In honor of Sloppy Joe's Bar in Key West (founded in 1933), and its proximity to Cuba, this cook sends her Cuban take on the classic sloppy joe. The flavors mirror a Cuban staple, picadillo, but the consistency stays true to the thick, creamy sloppy joes that emerged from it.

1 tsp. water

1/2 tsp. baking soda

2 tsp. salt, divided

1/2 lb. ground beef

1/2 lb. ground pork

1/4 cup extra-virgin olive oil

1 medium yellow onion, small dice

1 large green bell pepper, stemmed, cored, seeded, small dice

3 large garlic cloves, peeled and pressed

1/4 tsp. black pepper

1/2 tsp. ground cumin

1 tsp. dried oregano

2 Tbsp. tomato paste

1 cup tomato sauce (add more if the sauce looks too dry)

1/2 cup of diced tomatoes, roughly chopped

1/4 cup dry white wine

1/4 cup pimiento-stuffed green olives, minced

1/4 cup raisins, minced

1/2 Tbsp. flour

1 Tbsp. sherry wine vinegar or red wine vinegar

2 Tbsp. parsley, finely chopped

Optional:

1 tsp. coconut aminos

Mustard, Swiss cheese, and Cuban bread for serving

Dice the yellow onion and green bell pepper and place in a medium bowl. Peel and press the garlic cloves and add to the onion mixture. Stir.

Measure out 1 teaspoon salt, black pepper, ground cumin, and oregano and set aside in a small bowl.

Mince the olives and raisins and set aside.

Whisk water, baking soda, and the remaining 1 teaspoon of salt in a small bowl.

In a large bowl, add the ground beef and ground pork. Pour the baking soda mixture over the meat and gently mix with your hands to combine. This will help keep the meat moist while it cooks. Note: Be careful not to overmix so the meat doesn't toughen.

Heat the olive oil in a 13-inch skillet over medium heat until it begins to shimmer.

Once oil is heated, add the yellow onion mixture and spices to the pan and sauté until the onions are translucent, about 5–8 minutes.

Add tomato paste to the vegetables and stir to combine. Continue to cook, stirring continuously, for an additional 2 minutes.

Move sautéed vegetables to the border of the pan, leaving a space in the center for the ground meat.

Add meat to the center of the pan and cook until evenly browned. Stir to break apart any large chunks of meat. Cook until most of the meat juice has evaporated.

Once the meat is browned and the mixture is thickened, add tomato sauce, diced tomatoes, wine, olives, and raisins.

Reduce heat to low and simmer, covered, for about 8 minutes. Stir occasionally.

Add 1 tablespoon flour and stir to thoroughly distribute. This should thicken the mixture. Cook for 1–2 more minutes. Meanwhile, chop the parsley.

Once the meat is cooked, add vinegar and fresh parsley. Stir to combine. Taste and adjust seasoning as needed. Note: Normally sloppy joe mixtures include brown sugar. If you prefer a sweeter mixture, feel free to add coconut aminos to produce your desired sweetness level. I recommend 1 teaspoon.

Serve on hamburger bun. For an extra Cuban twist, use Cuban bread topped with Swiss cheese and yellow mustard.

Serves 6.

Pompano Amandine

Its delicate, especially fine-flavored flesh makes pompano Florida's "fish deluxe."

$1/2$ lb. pompano
$1/2$ stick butter
$1/4$ tsp. salt
Dash white pepper
2 Tbsp. slivered almonds
Lime wedges
Parsley

Clean pompano, but leave it whole, with the head on. Melt butter in small skillet, using enough to measure $1/4$ inch deep in the pan. Sauté fish until it flakes easily, 5–6 minutes on each side. Remove pompano to warmed serving dish; season with salt and pepper. In pan drippings, cook almonds until just pale golden. Pour butter-almond sauce over pompano. Garnish with lime and parsley. Serves 1.

"Coconutty" Recipes

Coconut delicacies are as traditional to Key West as widow's walks and Martello Towers. Fresh coconut cake is a Key West trademark. It was served to President Truman, President Eisenhower, Secretary of State John Foster Dulles, and countless other dignitaries who visited the island. Old-timers insist that freshly grated coconut must be used. One meltingly good taste and you will know how right they are! (Tip: Frozen grated coconut is the next best thing.)

. . .

Key West Coconut Cake

$1/4$ cup shortening
$11/2$ cup sugar
3 cups cake flour
4 tsp. baking powder
$1/2$ tsp. salt
1 cup coconut milk
1 tsp. vanilla extract

5 egg whites
2 Tbsp. cooking oil

Cream together shortening and sugar. Sift together flour, baking powder, and salt. Add alternately with coconut milk to creamed mixture. Add vanilla extract. Beat egg whites until stiff; fold into batter. Pour into 2 oiled 8 × 8 × 2-inch square layer pans or 2 oiled 9-inch layer pans. Bake in a 375°F oven 30 minutes. Cool 5 minutes. Remove layers from pans; cool on wire rack. When cool, fill and frost. Makes 1 cake.

Coconut Filling:
2 egg whites
1½ cups sugar
½ cup coconut milk
1 Tbsp. white corn syrup
½ tsp. salt
1 tsp. vanilla extract
1 coconut, grated

Combine all ingredients except vanilla and coconut. With electric mixer, beat at high speed about 1 minute to blend. Then place over rapidly boiling water, using mixer to beat continuously until firm peaks form, about 8 minutes. Remove from heat, turn into bowl, and add vanilla extract. Fill and frost cooled cake layers, sprinkling generously with grated coconut.

· · ·

Coconut Cookie Balls

2 egg whites
1 cup sugar
1 Tbsp. flour
2 cups grated coconut
1 tsp. vanilla extract

Beat egg whites until stiff. Beat in sugar, a little at a time; then beat in flour. Blend in coconut and vanilla. Drop by teaspoons onto well-greased cookie sheet. Bake in 350°F oven about 18 minutes or until lightly browned.

Remove from pan at once. Makes about 30 cookies.

···

Queen of All Puddings

British influence is evident in this rich pudding, brought to Key West from the Bahama Islands. Duffs, trifles, tarts, and other puddings are also attributable to the British.

1 quart milk, scalded
2 cups soft bread crumbs
3 egg yolks
1/4 cup sugar
2 Tbsp. butter
1/2 cup guava jelly
3 egg whites
6 Tbsp. sugar
Flaked coconut

Pour scalded milk over breadcrumbs; cool. Beat egg yolks lightly with 1/4 cup sugar; add to milk and breadcrumbs. Melt butter in a deep baking dish. Add butter to custard, then pour custard into baking dish. Preheat oven to 350°F; place pudding in oven in pan of warm water. Bake 1 hour 15 minutes, or until silver knife inserted in center comes out clean. When pudding has set, remove from oven and spread top with guava jelly. Beat egg whites until foamy, gradually adding sugar until peaks form. Swirl on top; sprinkle with coconut. Bake in 350°F oven 12–15 minutes, until lightly browned. Serves 4–6.

···

Coconut Chicken Salad

1 cup chopped cooked chicken
1 cup diced celery
1/2 cup grated coconut
1/2 cup green seedless grapes
1/4 cup chopped pecans or walnuts
Salt to taste
1/2 cup mayonnaise, thinned with a little cream
1 ripe avocado
1 lime

Prepare chicken, celery, coconut, grapes, and nuts. Combine. Add salt; mix with mayonnaise. Chill. Cut avocado in half; rub lime on front to prevent darkening. When ready to serve, fill avocado halves with chicken salad. Serves 2.

Other Tropical Fruit Recipes

...

The Original Key Lime Pie

The Key Lime Pie originated by pioneer settlers of the Florida Keys has gained worldwide recognition. Because they lacked refrigeration, the islanders relied on sweetened condensed milk. Here is the original recipe, plus two delicious variations.

6 egg yolks, beaten slightly
1 15-oz. can sweetened condensed milk
1/2 cup Key lime juice (or Persian lime)
1 9-inch baked pie shell, pastry or crumb
6 egg whites, stiffly beaten
4 Tbsp. sugar

Combine egg yolks and condensed milk. Mix well. Add lime juice; blend well. Turn into baked pie shell. Beat egg whites until stiff peaks form, gradually adding sugar. Swirl onto pie, spreading to edge of pie shell all around. Bake in 300°F oven until meringue is pale honey-colored.

...

Frozen Lime Pie

1/2 cup Key lime or Persian lime juice
1 15-oz. can sweetened condensed milk
5 egg whites
2 Tbsp. sugar
1 Tbsp. grated lemon rind
Few drops green food coloring
1 9-inch graham cracker pie shell

Combine lime juice and condensed milk, stirring until thick and smooth. Beat egg whites until foamy. Add sugar, one tablespoon at a time, and continue beating until stiff. Add food color. Fold in lime-milk mixture. Sprinkle lemon rind on bottom of pie shell; turn filling into shell. Chill until set. Freeze and keep until time to serve or serve without freezing. For topping, swirl on sweetened whipped cream. (For instructions, see Whipped Cream Frosting, page 105.)

Lime Sour or Old Sour

This potent mixture is a great favorite in the Florida Keys. Natives like it on seafood cocktail, seafood salad, or broiled, baked, or fried fish:

Strain 1 pint Key lime juice from ripe, yellow limes into a bottle. Add 1 tablespoon salt and cork tightly. Let stand at room temperature until fermented—two to four weeks. The Bahamians brought this condiment to the Keys.

. . .

Lime Chiffon Pie

1 envelope unflavored gelatin
1/4 cup cold water
3 eggs, separated
1 cup sugar, divided
1/2 cup lime juice
1/4 tsp. salt
Green food coloring
1 tsp. grated lemon peel
1 cup heavy cream, whipped
1 baked 9-inch pie shell

Soften gelatin in cold water. In top of double boiler, beat egg yolks slightly. Add 2/3 cup sugar, lime juice, and salt. Cook over hot water until thick, stirring constantly; remove from heat. Stir in softened gelatin until thoroughly dissolved. Tint pale green with food coloring. Chill until slightly thickened. Beat egg whites until stiff but not dry. Gradually beat in remaining 1/3 cup sugar and grated lemon peel. Fold into gelatin mixture, then fold in half of whipped cream. Pile into cooled pie shell; chill until firm. Swirl remaining whipped cream onto top of pie. Refrigerate until ready to serve.

...

Guacamole

Tip: If guacamole must stand for some time, put it in the refrigerator with an avocado pit in the center and it will not darken.

2 ripe avocados
Juice of 1 lime
1/2 tsp. salt
1/2 tsp. chili powder
2 tsp. fresh onion juice
4 drops red hot sauce
1/2 of 3-oz. package cream cheese
1 Tbsp. minced pimiento (optional)

Peel avocados, remove pits, and mash with silver fork to prevent darkening. Add lime juice, then blend in seasonings and cream cheese. If pimiento is used, stir it in last. Use as a dip with potato chips, or stuff tomatoes for salad. Spread on toast or top a quesadilla with it.

...

Caribbean Guava Punch

2 quarts Jamaican rum
1 1/2 cups Key lime juice
2 1/4 lbs. sugar
2 quarts strong tea
1 quart sweet sherry
2 quarts water
1 lb. guava jelly
1/2 pint brandy
3 quarts ginger ale

Mix all ingredients except ginger ale in large punch bowl, well iced. Just before serving time, add ginger ale.

...

Tropical Dessert Sauce

1 5-oz. can evaporated milk
2/3 cup sugar
1/2 tsp. almond extract
Juice of 2 Key limes

A sauce in the Keys tradition, great over Jell-o or ice cream.

Chill milk; beat with electric mixer until foamy. Add sugar; whip again. Squeeze limes, strain juice. Add almond extract and juice. Tangy but sweet, this has the consistency of whipped cream. Makes 1¼ cups.

Cuban Coffee

The following excerpt from *Key West Recipes* by Luise Putcamp and Virginia Z. Goult published in 1948 describes the Cuban coffee tradition during that time. Cuban coffee has maintained and increased in popularity throughout the state.

Some Key Westers begin their days early in the morning with a cup of Cuban coffee, and a piece of bread. Sometimes this is breakfast enough. Others have their coffee first and about 8 o'clock have a real breakfast of more coffee, boiled or fried fish and grits, and a dish of raw or stewed fruit. . . .

Five or six times a day coffee is served. Not much at a time—about half a cupful, which the Cubans call "un buchito" (a mouthful) and which most everyone else calls a "bouchie." Cuban coffee is roasted almost to the point of being burned, and then is very finely ground.

The best coffee makers put the coffee into a flannel bag, pour on the hot water, and let it filter through slowly. The bag is suspended from an iron three-legged tripod, and the coffee is dripped into whichever kind of vessel you prefer, providing it can be put back on the stove and reheated as often as is necessary. The flannel bag is then washed carefully and hung in the sun by the kitchen door to dry. That is the traditional way to make coffee.

Sunny Gulf Coast

*Spanish pirates once rode the waves where now a peaceful
sailboat regatta drifts across Tampa Bay off St. Petersburg.*

Tampa is the name of the Calusa Indian town shown on 1580 maps. Fifty-two years before that, Panfilo de Narvaez, commissioned governor of Florida, had come to the Tampa Bay area and taken a party of men inland to explore. They ended the expedition in St. Mark's, Florida. He was followed in 1539 by Hernando de Soto, who came ashore and struggled against the local native peoples.

The first North American settlement was a log fort built in 1823. By the time of the War Between the States, Tampa's vast pastures were filled with cattle and trade was brisk with Cuba.

When four companies moved out to join the Confederate Army, the defenseless town was blockaded and shelled in 1863 and later occupied by federal forces. The city was in desperate condition after the war when yellow fever swept through the area.

Progress did not really begin until 1884, when Henry B. Plant brought the railroad to Tampa. The Plant System of rails had a hub in Sanford, Florida, and one in Waycross, Georgia. Then, Port Tampa was a small harbor. Plant extended rail service nine miles from Tampa to the port. He developed it into a deep-water port thus securing Tampa as a major international shipping hub. Meanwhile, phosphate had been discovered and mining began in Alachua County, near Hawthorne, in 1883. Used primarily as fertilizer for food production, a lively phosphate industry sprang up.

Meanwhile, Spanish-born Vicente Martinez Ybor brought his cigar factory from Key West in 1885. He liked the port access there for cigar shipment and worker ease of movement and bought 40 acres. Thousands of workers—Cubans, Afro-Cubans, Spaniards, and Italians—worked together in cigar factories and lived in the same community during a time of segregation in the U.S. South. Women worked alongside men rolling cigars. By 1900, Ybor City was the world's cigar capital.

And Henry B. Plant built the huge Tampa Bay Hotel, hoping to outdo Henry Flagler's east coast success. It became U.S. Army headquarters during the Spanish-American War, and Colonel Theodore Roosevelt trained his Rough Riders in the hotel's backyard. There was another great epidemic, this time of typhoid fever, and troops were tended by Clara Barton, founder of the Red Cross.

After the war's end, Tampa again thrived as a result of high-class, handmade Havana cigars. The boom period saw hotels and apartments built, also the Gandy Bridge that spanned Tampa Bay and connected the city with St. Petersburg.

This fine natural port made it choice for concentrated action during World War II, and shipbuilding gave jobs to thousands. Another aid to community growth was MacDill Air Force Base.

Tampa thrived until the mid-1900s when the tobacco embargo caused the industry to move to Central America. The historic 110-block area of cigar factories has come to life again, with deserted buildings converted to restaurants, art galleries, and boutiques.

Tampa's airport, one of the nation's finest, is the destination of many tourists who then make the short drive to Disney World. Also, it's worth the drive to see the spectacular Skyway Bridge linking Tampa and St. Petersburg with South Florida.

Each February swashbuckling "pirates" reinvade Tampa via the world's only fully rigged pirate ship during the annual Gasparilla Pirate Festival. This duplicates the invasion of Jose Gaspar, a nineteenth-century buccaneer. Since 1904 the festival celebrates his spirit. While his existence has not been proven, legend tells he was a Spanish lieutenant who stole a ship in Cuba and sailed to the area to hide in the bays and inlets of the Gulf Coast. After 30 years, on the way to retirement in South America, he wanted one more prize. Unfortunately, as the legend goes, it was a U.S. Navy ship and battle ensued. He wrapped a chain around his waist and jumped into the sea, preferring death to confinement.

While Southern cooking holds first place among longtime Floridians, Spanish-Cuban restaurants like the world-famous Columbia Restaurant in Ybor City, established in 1905, have spiced local menus with Latin flavor. Party fare is likely to feature garbanzo bean soup, arroz con pollo, and fresh Dixie coconut cake. The Columbia is the oldest continuously operated restaurant in Florida. Others are now in Clearwater, Sarasota, St. Augustine, and Celebration.

Population has soared along the Gulf Coast. Fortunately, the Ten Thousand Islands remains a protected area, known for its vast beauty and great fishing. Sleepy little Marco Island is now studded with waterfront hotels. Naples, with luxury estates and upscale shopping, is known as the Palm Beach of the west coast. And Sarasota, with its opera, ballet, artists' colony, and circus history, is a haven for sun-seeking retirees.

The entire coast is a land of white sugar beaches strewn with beautiful seashells and lazy rivers that join streams with the blue Gulf—an ideal area for boating and fishing.

In 1887, 25 miles northwest of Tampa, Tarpon Springs was incorporated into a city. Today, it has the largest percentage of Americans with Greek heritage of any city in the United States. This Greek community was settled during the 1880s by sponge fishermen lured from their homeland to the bountiful west coast sponge beds.

In colorful religious ceremonies to celebrate Epiphany, the sponge fleet is blessed each January 6 and young men dive for the golden cross flung into the Spring Bayou by the archbishop. Even more exciting is the Greek food—savory, herb-blessed lamb, sweet stone crab claws, stuffed grape leaves, and a salad that is a work of art.

The Tarpon Springs historic Greektown district was added to the National Register of Historic Places as a Traditional Culture Property, the first with this designation in a Florida community. Agriculture is big business along this coast and inland, providing plenty of locally produced citrus and beef, garden vegetables, guavas, watermelons, and berries. With seafood plentiful, local cooks do great things with shrimp and crabmeat, lobster and fish.

Southern Styles

...

Baked Snook

Courtesy of Jorge Lara

2 to 4 snook fillets, no thicker than 1 inch
Butter
Mayonnaise
Olive oil
Parmesan cheese, grated
Capers

Preheat the oven to 350°F. As it preheats, get a baking pan and line with aluminum foil. Use olive oil to lightly grease it to avoid fish sticking.

Take each fillet and, using a rubber spatula, apply a light coat of mayonnaise on both sides until it is completely coated. This helps the grated cheese to stick. Generously sprinkle the cheese on both sides of the fillet. Repeat for all fillets.

Place them on the baking pan. Cut butter into squares the diameter and thickness of quarters and place on fillets. Sprinkle capers on top.

Bake for 18 to 20 minutes. Check the fillets at 18 minutes by cutting into one with a fork. If the fork cuts through without effort, it is ready. If not, do not leave the fillets more than 2 minutes and then repeat the fork test.

Knives are not required if fish is cooked properly.

Now at the Isles of Capri Fire and Rescue Station and living in Naples, Lieutenant Jorge Lara once lived in nearby Everglades City and worked as a firefighter. With 24 hours on the job and 48 hours off, he spent much of this free time fishing and exploring the area—from Pavilion Key to Shark River on a 16-foot flats boat. Snook is not commercially fished. Yet it is caught during the right seasons in the Atlantic and Gulf of Mexico, including Everglades National Park and Monroe County.

• • •

Alzilia's Eggplant

Courtesy of Anne Smathers

1½ pounds peeled eggplant, chopped into ½ inch cubes
¾ cup grated sharp cheddar cheese
4 oz. blue cheese, crumbled
1 egg, beaten
Crumbled crackers (Ritz or similar texture), optional
Dots of butter
1½ teaspoons salt

Boil peeled and chopped eggplant in a large pot of salted water for 15–20 minutes. Drain in colander. Mix eggplant with the two cheeses and beaten egg. Put in small, greased casserole. Add crumbled crackers on top and dot with butter. Bake at 325°F for 30 minutes.

Alzilia Fitzgerald Cooper cooked for the Smathers family during World War II in Mississippi. Lacking enough cheddar cheese for the recipe, she added blue cheese, creating a dish the family loved. The recipe traveled with the family to Tampa and remains a favorite across generations.

• • •

Ceviche Basics

Courtesy of Jacobo Jones

2 lbs. fresh shrimp or fish or other seafood, using the freshest possible.
   If using shrimp, peel and devein before using

1/2 cup lemon juice
1/2 cup lime juice
1/4 cup chopped cilantro
2 Tbsp. extra virgin olive oil
1 medium red onion, sliced thin
Salt and pepper to taste
Optional ingredients:
Herbs that pair well with fish (e.g., tarragon, dill, parsley, fennel fronds)
Vegetables/fruits that may be added (orange slices, tomatoes, avocado, shallot)
Sometimes roasted pumpkin seeds (*pepitas*) are used to garnish or fried green plantain strips (*tajadas*).
Florida sweet potatoes, tomatoes, or other seasonal produce may be added.
Heat can be added with diced or sliced hot peppers of your choosing.

Prepare fish by cutting into small bite size pieces (1/4-inch to 1/2-inch cubes works well). If using shrimp, cut into pieces depending on size.

Combine all ingredients in a bowl and toss thoroughly to coat fish with citrus juices.

Refrigerate for at least one hour or longer, until fish is thoroughly "cooked" through and the color is opaque. The acidity of the citrus juices coagulates the proteins of the fish, "cooking" it without heat.

Serve as is, or on a bed of lettuce, with crackers or toast points. Serves 4–8 as an appetizer or main dish.

Ceviche can be made with almost any fresh fish. While the recipe hails from Peru, Floridians have adapted it using local, fresh-caught fish and shrimp. Scallops may also be used. The seafood's freshness is key.

Ybor City Specialties

La Segunda Central Bakery

Catalan-born Juan More fought in the Spanish-American War in Cuba, where he came to love Cuban bread. He found a traditional recipe for it and brought it to Tampa. At the start of World War I, he joined a co-op of bakers and cigar-makers to open three bakeries in Tampa: La Primera, La Segunda, and La Tercera. When two closed, More bought La Segunda from his partners, establishing it as his own in 1915. Still in Ybor City, it is Tampa's oldest bakery.

The bread recipe is unchanged. In line with traditional methods, bakers place a fresh palmetto leaf across the top of the 3-foot-long loaves to keep moisture in while baking. This also creates a signature light split down the middle of the loaf when removed before eating.

In a recent *Forum* magazine article, Dalia Colon writes the bakery produces 20,000 loaves daily. Shipments go as far as Alaska and "perhaps even more unbelievably, to Miami."

La Segunda recently expanded by adding locations in South Tampa and in St. Petersburg.

. . .

Tender-Crust Cuban Bread

1½ package active dry yeast
2⅔ cups warm water
1¼ Tbsp. salt
1¼ Tbsp. sugar
8 cups sifted all-purpose flour
¼ cup yellow cornmeal
¼ cup melted butter or margarine

Dissolve yeast in ⅔ cups warm water until soft. Add salt, sugar, and remaining 2 cups warm water, stirring thoroughly. Add flour a cup at a time, beating it in with a wooden spoon. Working on a lightly floured board, knead dough for about 15 minutes, until it is smooth and elastic. Place in a large, well-oiled bowl, brush top with melted butter, and cover with a tea towel. Set in a warm place for about one hour, until dough doubles in size. Punch dough down with your fist. Again on lightly floured board, shape dough into two long, narrow loaves. Sprinkle cookie sheet with cornmeal and place loaves on it. Cut several slashes in top. Let rise 5 minutes. Brush tops with melted butter and place in cold oven. Turn oven to 400°F and bake 45 minutes or until loaves are golden brown. Place pan of boiling water in oven during baking time. Remove bread from oven, and again brush it with melted butter. Makes 2 loaves, golden crusted outside, light and snowy inside.

. . .

Florida Mullet with Spanish Sauce

1 3-lb. mullet (or red snapper)
Salt and pepper
Flour
6 Tbsp. melted butter
1/4 cup chopped onion
2 cups chopped celery
1/4 cup chopped green pepper
3 cups canned tomatoes
1 tsp. Worcestershire sauce
1 Tbsp. ketchup
1/2 tsp. chili powder
1/2 lemon, thinly sliced
1 bay leaf
1 clove minced garlic
1 tsp. salt
1 tsp. sugar
Dash cayenne pepper

Mix flour, salt, and pepper and coat mullet inside and out. Melt butter in skillet and over low heat, cook onion, celery, and green pepper in butter for 15 minutes. Add all remaining ingredients and simmer until celery is tender. Press mixture through potato ricer; pour sauce over cleaned fish and bake in 350°F oven 45 minutes, basting frequently with Spanish sauce. Serves 4 generously.

Spanish Bean Soup

From the famous Columbia Restaurant

1/2 lb. dried garbanzo beans
10 cups water
1 Tbsp. salt
1 beef bone
Ham bone
2 quarts water
1/4 lb. salt pork, chopped fine
Pinch paprika
1 Tbsp. shortening
1 chopped onion
1 lb. potatoes, peeled and quartered
1 pinch saffron
1 chorizo (Spanish sausage), cut in thin slices

Place beans in salted water in a large pot, to soak overnight. Next day, drain water and place beans, beef and ham bones, and 2 quarts water in a large pot. Place over low heat; simmer 45 minutes. Fry the chopped salt pork, add paprika and onion (plus 1 tablespoon shortening if needed), and cook until onion is tender. Add to beans, then add potatoes. Toast saffron on the cover of a casserole or in the oven and mash before measuring. Mix it with a little hot stock from the pot, then add it to the soup. Taste and season with salt and pepper. When the potatoes are done, put chorizo slices in the soup and serve it hot. Serves 4.

Chicken and Yellow Rice Valenciana

1 2 1/2-lb. frying chicken, quartered
1/2 cup fresh olive oil
2 chopped onions
1 chopped green pepper
1 clove garlic, chopped fine
2 Tbsp. salt
1 bay leaf
Small can tomatoes, drained
1/4 tsp. pepper
2 1/2 cups Valencia or pearl rice

Chicken and Yellow Rice Valenciana is an Ybor City Specialty.

5 cups water
2 chicken bouillon cubes
$\frac{1}{2}$ cup sherry wine (optional)
$\frac{1}{8}$ tsp. saffron
1 cup green peas
1 dozen green olives
1 small jar pimientos

Brown chicken in olive oil over medium heat. Remove chicken from pan.
Add onions, green pepper, and garlic. Continue cooking until slightly
brown, about 5 minutes. Return chicken to pot and stir in salt, bay leaf,
tomatoes, and pepper. Add rice, water in which 2 chicken bouillon cubes
have been dissolved, and wine. Dissolve saffron in small amount of water
and add (or use a few drops of yellow food coloring mixed with water).
Bring to a boil. Bake in preheated oven at 350°F for 20 minutes. Garnish
with green peas, olives, and pimientos. Serves 4.

Italians

Italians—mostly from Sicily—worked in Tampa's cigar industry.
The U.S. Census in 1900 shows 1,315 Italians lived in Ybor City's
eastern district, which eventually came to be dubbed "Little Italy."

In more contemporary times, Tampa, Miami, and Key West have
debated over the birthplace of the Cuban sandwich. Tampa's version
contains Genoa salami, as a result of the Italian population. People
who were raised with the Key West or Miami versions are advocates
of their versions as the original.

. . .

JoJo's Easy Shrimp, Mushroom, & Artichoke Casserole

Courtesy of JoJo Versaggi

7 Tbsp. butter
$\frac{1}{2}$ lb. mushrooms, large can
$1\frac{1}{2}$ lbs. shrimp, shelled and deveined
1 large can artichoke hearts

4½ Tbsp. flour
¼ cup milk
¾ cup heavy cream
½ cup dry sherry
1 Tbsp. Worcestershire sauce
½ cup Parmesan cheese
Salt, pepper, paprika

In a skillet, melt 2½ tablespoons butter and sauté the mushrooms. Set aside in a bowl. Add shrimp to skillet and cook for about one minute until it starts to turn pink.

Take a 2-quart casserole and layer artichokes, mushrooms, and shrimp. Set aside.

In a saucepan, melt the remaining butter. Add flour and stir with a wire whisk. Gradually add milk and cream, stirring until thick. Add sherry, Worcestershire, salt, and pepper. Pour mixture over casserole. Sprinkle with grated cheese. Add paprika for color. Bake at 375°F for 20 to 30 minutes.

Though largely associated with Italian immigrant leadership in the shrimping industry on the First Coast, the Versaggi family maintains operations in Tampa.

• • •

Virgil's Shrimp Cakes

Courtesy of Janis Versaggi Williams

2 long green onions, chopped fine
10–12 sprigs parsley, chopped fine
10–12 garlic cloves, minced
1 fresh cayenne pepper (two if you're brave), minced
2 lbs. raw shrimp, clean and cut into ¼-inch pieces
2 cups all-purpose flour
2 Tbsp. baking powder
2 cups cold water
Oil for frying
Salt to taste

Mix flour, water, and baking powder together in a bowl until all lumps disappear. Add the remaining ingredients and mix thoroughly, then chill in the refrigerator until firm. Using a tablespoon, drop mixture into 325°F deep fryer until cakes are fully cooked (about 4–5 minutes). Goes well with soy sauce. Serves 6.

. . .

Shrimp Quiche

Courtesy of Bernadette Versaggi

Crust: Make your own or buy ready-made crust and follow package directions.

Filling:
4 eggs
1 lb. shrimp, jumbo for easy peeling
Swiss or Monterey Jack cheese
1 cup milk
1–2 Tbsp. all-purpose flour
Salt, pepper to taste
1/2 onion, finely chopped
1 pkg. frozen spinach

Follow directions for crust. Break eggs, separating yolks and whites. Brush whites on crust with a pastry brush. Pre-cook and peel shrimp (don't cook all the way). Cut into bite-size pieces. Grate cheese. Cook spinach according to package directions. Add eggs, flour, salt, and pepper to a bowl and beat with a wire whisk.

Layer the ingredients by lining the pie shell with shrimp pieces, then onion, then spinach. Pour the egg mixture into pie. Top with cheese.

Preheat oven to 425°F. Cook the quiche for 15 minutes at this temperature, then lower heat to 300°F and cook for 45 more minutes or until knife comes out clean. Let cool 10 minutes before serving. Serves 6–8.

. . .

Mock Oyster Casserole

*Created by Emilio Longo, Italian American
from New York to Florida in 1948.*

Courtesy of the Longo Family

1 medium eggplant
1 7-oz. can minced clams, save juice
Cream, enough to make one cup with clam juice
1 Tbsp. flour
1 Tbsp. chopped parsley
1 Tbsp. butter
1 Tbsp. minced onions
Buttered bread crumbs

Peel eggplant, then cut into good-sized chunks. Cook in boiling salted water until tender, about 10 minutes.

Drain the clams and reserve liquid. Add cream to the clam liquid to make 1 cup.

Melt the butter. Add onion and sauté lightly. Stir in the flour. Add clam liquid and cream gradually, stirring until thickened slightly.

Stir in clams. Fold in drained eggplant and parsley. Place in buttered baking dish. Top with buttered breadcrumbs. Bake in moderate oven at 350°F for ¹/₂ hour or until brown.

· · ·

Delivery Chicken

Courtesy of Captain Mel Longo

1 whole chicken, fryer or roaster
4 onions, cut into quarters
3 potatoes, cut into quarters
1–2 cups Progresso Italian breadcrumbs (depends on chicken size)
¹/₂ stick of butter
1 clove crushed garlic
¹/₂ cup fresh mushrooms, sliced
¹/₃ cup chopped pecans
Handful of raisins
¹/₃ cup orange juice

A simple chicken dish created at sea in order to feed his crew.

Melt the butter in a saucepan and cook garlic and mushrooms. Add breadcrumbs, raisins, orange juice, and pecans and mix. Stuff this into the chicken's cavity. Rub the chicken with butter, then salt and pepper it. Place orange slices on top if available. Put the chicken into the baking dish surrounded by onions and potatoes and bake at 350°F.

Baste every 10 minutes or so. The chicken is done when internal temperature is 165 or when it doesn't bleed when you cut it to the bone or when a leg falls off.

Greek Dishes

. . .

Lamb Kebobs, Greek Style

1/2 tsp. Tabasco
1/8 tsp. basil
1/2 cup olive or salad oil
1/4 cup lime or lemon juice
1/4 cup red wine, optional
1 Tbsp. onion juice
1 tsp. dry mustard
1/2 tsp. salt
1/8 tsp. thyme
2 lbs. boneless lamb shoulder, cut in 1 1/2-inch cubes
1 green pepper, cut in 1-inch pieces
3 tomatoes, quartered
12 small whole onions

Blend Tabasco, oil, lime juice, wine, and onion juice in bowl. Add dry mustard, salt, basil, and thyme. Add meat cubes. (Beef chuck may be substituted, but if used should be sprinkled with meat tenderizer.) Let stand 5 hours or overnight in refrigerator. Alternate meat and vegetables on skewers. Place in preheated broiler or on grill about 4 inches from heat. Broil approximately 10 minutes on each side. Serve with rice pilaf. Serves 6.

. . .

Louis Pappas' Famous Greek Salad

1 large head lettuce
3 cups potato salad (see below)
12 sprigs watercress
2 tomatoes, cut into 6 wedges each

1 peeled cucumber, cut into 8 long fingers
1 peeled avocado, cut into wedges
4 portions of Feta cheese
1 green pepper, cut into 8 rings
4 slices canned cooked beets

Potato salad:
6 boiled potatoes, sliced and cooled
2 medium onions, chopped
1/4 cup finely chopped parsley
4 peeled, cooked shrimp
4 anchovy fillets
12 Greek black olives
4 radishes, cut like roses
4 whole green onions
1/2 cup distilled white vinegar
1/4 cup each olive and salad oil, blended
Oregano
Salt to taste
1/2 cup thinly sliced green onion
1/2 cup salad dressing

Save 10 outside lettuce leaves and shred remaining lettuce finely. Prepare all vegetables as indicated above. Spread whole lettuce leaves on a platter. In the center, mound potato salad and cover it with shredded lettuce, then watercress. Alternate tomato wedges and cucumber fingers around outside of platter; circle with avocado slices. Atop the salad, arrange the slices of Feta cheese, green pepper slices, olives, peppers, and green onions. Finally, top the salad with beet slices, shrimp, and anchovy fillets. Sprinkle with vinegar and blended oils, then with oregano. Serve at once with toasted Greek garlic bread. Serves 4.

Served at Louis Pappas Restaurant in Tarpon Springs, this salad has influenced Greek salads in the Tampa Bay area. However, it is atypical of Greek salads as a result of the potato salad being included. The origin of that modification is debated.

•••

Moussaka Potatoes with Beef

1/2 clove garlic, chopped
1/2 cup oil for frying, preferably olive oil
6–8 medium potatoes, sliced
1 large onion, chopped
1 lb. ground beef (or lamb)
1 tsp. salt
1/4 tsp. pepper
Pinch cinnamon
Pinch sugar
1 cup water
1/4 cup dry red wine
2 cans tomato sauce, heated
2 bay leaves

While this dish is better known for using eggplant, it is also made with potatoes.

Lightly brown garlic in oil; remove. Sauté potatoes in oil until light brown but not done. Set potatoes aside. Mix meat, onion, garlic, salt, and pepper to taste. Fry for 3 minutes. Spread meat mixture between layers of potatoes in oiled baking dish, starting and ending with potatoes. Combine wine, water, tomato sauce, cinnamon, and sugar. Place bay leaves atop casserole and pour over all the wine liquid. Bake in 350°F oven 45 to 60 minutes. Remove bay leaves before serving hot. Serves 6.

•••

Greek Chicken Avgolemono Soup with Orzo

By Themelina Tsikouris
Courtesy of Maria Kouskoutis

6 chicken pieces
1 onion, chopped
1 rib of celery, chopped
1 carrot, chopped
1 small potato, grated
1 Tbsp. salt
1/4 tsp. black pepper
3/4 cup orzo or rice

Wash chicken and place in a pot. Add enough water so water level is about 3 inches above chicken. Gather froth from the surface as the water begins to heat. Add onion, celery, carrot, potato, salt, and pepper. Allow chicken to cook for about 45–60 minutes. Remove chicken pieces once cooked. Skim fat from surface. (Optional: Remove vegetables, mash or blend, and return to pot.) Add orzo (or rice) to soup and cook according to package directions. De-bone chicken, cut into desired chunks or shred, and add to soup.

Avgo-Lemono Sauce:
Whisk 1 egg white. Add the yolk and the juice of one lemon.

Continue whisking as you slowly drizzle warm-hot soup into the egg-lemon mixture, until tempered.

Pour egg-lemon mixture into soup pot, stirring quickly to incorporate.

· · ·

Greek Honey Cakes

(Melomacarona)

2 cups salad oil
1/4 lb. butter
1/2 cup sugar
1/2 cup orange juice
5 cups sifted flour
3 tsp. baking powder
1/4 cup water
1 cup finely chopped walnuts
1/2 tsp. cinnamon
1/8 tsp. ground cloves

Syrup:
1/8 cup rum
1 lb. honey
1/4 cup warm water
1/2 cup finely chopped walnuts, for topping

Stir until blended oil, butter, and sugar; stir in orange juice then flour and mix until smooth. Quickly mix baking powder with 1/4 cup water and stir at once into dough. Mix in 1 cup walnuts, cinnamon, and cloves. Shape dough into cakes 3 × 1 1/2-inch. Bake on ungreased cookie sheet in 350°F oven 20 to 25 minutes. Cool on wire rack. Warm honey and mix with rum and ¼ cup warm water. Dip cool cakes into honey, sprinkle with chopped walnuts, and drain on rack over waxed paper. Makes about 24.

Tropical Fruit Recipes

. . .

Hot Wine Orange Punch

Juice of 1 orange
1½ cups water
½ cup. sugar
1 bottle red wine

In one saucepan, heat water and half of juice squeezed from orange. In another pan, dissolve sugar with remaining juice. Combine; boil 10 minutes. Heat red wine until it bubbles; pour in the orange-sugar mixture. Serve hot with thin slices of orange floating on top. A stimulating cold weather drink! Serves 6.

. . .

Dixie Coconut Cake

3 cups sifted cake flour
2 tsp. double-acting baking powder
½ tsp. salt
½ cup butter
1½ cups sugar
1 cup shredded coconut
1 cup water
1½ tsp. lemon extract
4 egg whites, stiffly beaten

Coconut is baked in the cake layers and used in frosting.

Sift flour once, measure, add baking powder and salt; sift twice more.

Cream butter until smooth, gradually adding sugar and creaming until soft and fluffy. To this, add coconut, then flour, then water, a little each time, beating well after each addition. When batter is smooth, stir in lemon extract; fold in egg whites, which should be quite stiff. Bake in 2 greased loaf pans 8 × 4 inches at 350°F for 1 hour and 15 minutes. Frost top and sides with Coconut Seven-Minute Frosting (see following).

Coconut Seven-Minute Frosting

2 unbeaten egg whites
1½ cups sugar
5 Tbsp. cold water
1½ tsp. light corn syrup
1 tsp. vanilla
1 cup lightly toasted coconut

In upper double boiler, combine egg whites, sugar, water, and corn syrup; beat with rotary eggbeater until well mixed. Place over rapidly boiling water and continue beating. Cook 7 minutes or until frosting stands in peaks.

Remove from heat, add vanilla, beat until thick. Spread on cake, and sprinkle with toasted coconut. Makes enough to frost a two-layer cake, including top and sides.

Pineapple Drop Cookies

1 cup light brown sugar
½ cup shortening mixed with butter
1 unbeaten egg
1 tsp. vanilla
¾ cup crushed pineapple
2 cups sifted all-purpose flour
1 tsp. baking powder
½ tsp. salt
½ tsp. baking soda
¼ cup chopped walnuts
½ cup raisins

Heat oven to 375°F. Stir together sugar, shortening, egg, and vanilla until blended. Spoon pineapple from can with as little syrup as possible into measuring cup and add. Stir in sifted dry ingredients, then walnuts and raisins. Drop by heaping teaspoonfuls on ungreased cookie sheet. Bake at 375°F for 12 minutes until lightly browned. Makes 36.

Florida Fruit Cake

1 cup salad oil
1 1/2 cups brown sugar
4 eggs
3 cups sifted flour
1 tsp. baking powder
2 tsp. salt
1 tsp. ground cloves
1 cup orange juice
1 cup chopped candied pineapple
2 cups candied cherries, halved
1 1/2 cups seedless raisins
1 cup chopped dates
2 Tbsp. peach brandy

In large bowl, beat oil, sugar, and eggs 2 minutes. Sift together 2 cups flour with baking powder, salt, and spices. Stir into oil mixture with orange juice. Mix remaining cup of flour with fruits and nuts. Combine with batter and mix thoroughly. Pour batter into two 9 × 5-inch loaf pans lined with greased brown paper. Bake in 275°F oven 2 1/2–3 hours. Remove and cool. Sprinkle brandy over cake, wrap, and store in cool place. Decorate with candied pineapple and cherries.

Makes 2 loaves.

Lime Pudding Cake

2 eggs, separated
1/4 cup sugar, divided
3 Tbsp. lime juice
1 tsp. grated lime rind
3 Tbsp. flour
1/4 tsp. salt
1 cup milk

This dessert has crusty cake topping above, rich lime sauce beneath.

Beat egg whites, gradually adding 1/2 cup sugar, until stiff and glossy. Set aside. Beat egg yolks. Add lime juice and grated rind to egg yolks. Mix 1/4 cup sugar, flour, and salt together. Sprinkle over lime mixture and beat well. Add milk; blend well. Fold egg yolk mixture into beaten egg whites.

Pour into 6 greased custard cups. Set in shallow pan of water and bake in 350°F oven 35 minutes until firm. Serves 6.

...

Orange-Rum Cream Cake

1 1/4 cups sifted cake flour
1 Tbsp. baking powder
1/4 tsp. salt
1/2 cup shortening
1 cup sugar
8 beaten egg yolks
1 tsp. grated orange rind
1/2 cup milk

Have all ingredients at room temperature. Sift together twice flour, baking powder, and salt. Cream shortening until fluffy; gradually add sugar. Blend until mixture is creamy. Stir in egg yolks and orange rind until well mixed.

Alternately add dry ingredients and milk, beating after each addition. Turn into two greased 8-inch cake pans and bake in 350°F oven 30 minutes. Cool 10 minutes; turn onto cake rack. Fill with Orange-Rum Filling and frost with Whipped Cream Frosting.

Orange-Rum Filling
3 Tbsp. butter
1/4 tsp. grated orange rind
1 1/2 cup sifted confectioners' sugar, divided
Dash salt
2 Tbsp. orange juice
1 tsp. rum

Cream butter with orange rind. Gradually add 1/2 cup sugar, blending after each addition. Add salt; mix well. Add remaining sugar alternately with orange juice, beating until smooth after each addition. Blend in rum. Spread on cake layer.

Whipped Cream Frosting
1 cup heavy cream
1/2 tsp. vanilla
3 Tbsp. sifted confectioners' sugar

Whip heavy cream until stiff. Fold in vanilla and confectioners' sugar. Spread over cooled cake.

Sweet Things

...

Marshmallow Fudge Cake

A novel filling and so easy to do!

2²/₃ cups sifted cake flour
3¹/₂ tsp. baking powder
¹/₂ tsp. salt
2 cups sugar
1¹/₃ cup salad oil
2 eggs
1 cup milk
1 tsp. vanilla
2 oz. unsweetened chocolate
16 marshmallows, melted

Sift together twice flour, baking powder, salt, and sugar. Add oil, eggs, milk, vanilla, and chocolate; blend well then beat 2 minutes. Pour into two 8-inch square pans, greased and lined with waxed paper. Bake in 325°F oven 1 hour. Cool. Place marshmallows atop one layer and broil to lightly brown. Cool 15 minutes. Top with plain cake layer and cover with fudge frosting.

...

A tasty version with baked-on topping.

Quick Caramel Cake

2 cups cake flour
3 tsp. baking powder
1 tsp. salt
1¹/₄ cups sugar
¹/₂ cup shortening
¹/₄ cup milk
1¹/₂ tsp. vanilla
2 eggs

Topping:
2 egg whites
1 cup brown sugar
¹/₂ cup chopped pecans
¹/₂ cup shortening
¹/₄ cup milk
1¹/₂ tsp. vanilla
2 eggs

Let all ingredients stand at room temperature 45 minutes before use. To sifted flour, add baking powder, salt, sugar; sift again into large mixer bowl. Add shortening, milk, and vanilla. Beat 2 minutes with mixer at low speed. Add unbeaten eggs and beat 1 minute longer. Pour into greased 8¹/₂ × 13¹/₂-inch pan. Set aside. Clean mixer beaters and beat egg whites until stiff but not dry. Gradually add brown sugar; beat well. Spread atop cake; sprinkle with nuts and bake on center rack in 350°F oven 35 minutes. Makes 1 cake.

The Heartland

Spanish explorers never found gold in Florida, but they brought citrus—Florida's richest treasure.

Just a few hours by car takes you far from the glamour of the Gold Coast into Florida's quietly beautiful heartland, a world of beef cattle ranches, orange groves, and vegetable farms. To the north in Ocala, racing thoroughbreds are raised on the rolling green hills. History was made near Orlando, where Disney World opened in 1971, drawing young and old from all parts of the world.

Around Lake Okeechobee, rich black mucklands have been producing sugar cane in volume since 1929. Sugar cane came to the West Indies with Christopher Columbus. Florida's sugar cane industry, centered in Clewiston, became a giant when Castro's Cuba was cut out of the U.S. market; President Dwight D. Eisenhower slashed sugar imports from the island in 1960. Two years later, a total trade embargo was established by the John F. Kennedy administration. Then, Florida sugar cane became a prime supplier of the nation's needs. Today, it is the state's most extensive crop, with 440,000 acres planted around Lake Okeechobee, especially its southern half.

In this same region and on farms far down in Homestead south of Miami, a huge percentage of the nation's supply of winter vegetables grows. Two large Seminole Tribe of Florida Reservations are near the lake—Big Cypress 30 miles east of Immokalee and Brighton—36,000 acres on the northwest shore of Lake Okeechobee. The Seminoles are hardworking cowboys. Early on, they were skilled in herding and herd rotation and had close knowledge of the terrain. Today, they are one of Florida's top beef producers. But other ranchers account for most of Florida's beef cattle, which are produced in central and south-central areas, especially in Polk, Osceola, Hendry, Highlands, Hardee, DeSoto, Hillsborough, Okeechobee, and Glades counties.

From Punta Gorda to Kissimmee, cattle graze on the flat prairies. Levis, ten-gallon hats, and boots are the uniform of the day and rodeos feature exciting riding and roping in the true western tradition.

Kissimmee, called Cow Town, had the dubious honor of originating the first bar for men who did not want to get off their horses to drink. The ride-in bar was begun about 1870, ten years before the west adopted the idea.

Spanish explorers brought cattle into the state and their runaways turned wild, then were herded by the Native Americans. Records show that in 1775 the Seminoles worked a herd of 7,000 to 10,000 cattle on Paynes Prairie. The cattle's descendants, along with crossbreeds with northern European beef and dairy cattle, created the Florida Cracker Cattle. It is named for the Crackers who kept them.

During the second Spanish occupation of Florida, from 1784 to 1821, the Spanish gave land grants to homesteaders who stocked the ranges with cattle from Europe as well as herds driven down from the southern states. As the Seminoles retreated into the Everglades, cattle ranchers moved in behind them all along the Kissimmee River Valley.

White "humpbacked" Brahman cows were introduced in 1936 from Texas for their hardiness, resistance to insects, disease, heat, and the ability to live off sparse grasslands. They were improved by crossbreeding with Black Angus, Hereford, Santa Gertrudis, and others. In 2021 Florida came in tenth in the country for cow numbers with 929,000 head according to the U.S. Department of Agriculture. The most popular milk cow is the Holstein, but five other breeds also contribute to our dairy consumption. Okeechobee and Highlands counties have the largest numbers of cattle and calves.

By 1895, when Frederic Remington, the noted writer-painter, visited Florida, he described the Cracker cowboys as a wild-looking group with "long hair, broad-brimmed hat, and gun slung on hip." The wild west was no wilder than Florida in the nineteenth century. Cattle rustling was widespread; shootouts and stabbings were common. Ranchers did not venture out at night nor enter woods alone in some areas. Criminals would attack then flee deep into the Everglades' watery wilderness to hide. At last, outraged citizens called a halt and law and order were reestablished.

Throughout the heartland, steak and chops restaurants are popular. And the cowboys' campfire victuals are much enjoyed: fried white bacon or salt pork, grits, beans, biscuits or cold corn pone, and coffee boiled with the grounds until it is strong and black.

Moving north in the state, one enters a land that flows into gently rolling hills, dipping down to incredibly blue lakes and many freshwater springs. Ironically, the Spanish who failed in their search for Florida gold brought into the state the citrus seeds that were to produce its greatest treasure—oranges, grapefruit, lemons, and tangerines.

Because citrus was found to have medicinal value, Columbus was ordered to carry with him seeds of the first citrus trees to reach the New World. Scattered throughout the Antilles, orange trees flourished and covered some Caribbean islands. There are strong indications that Ponce

Florida Citrus Label Tour

To learn more about the citrus industry, take a driving tour designed by the Lake County Historical Society. The Lake County Citrus Label Tour is a cross-county driving trail with 12 stops between Umatilla and Clermont. At one time, there were more than 50 packing houses in the area. Their beautiful labels are featured. The 226-foot Citrus Tower at Clermont, built in 1956, is a tribute to Central Florida's citrus industry and remains a popular tourist attraction.

de León introduced oranges to the North American mainland when he discovered Florida in 1513.

Later, in 1539, Hernando de Soto planted more trees during his expedition to Florida. Spanish law required that each sailor bound for America carry one hundred seeds but because the seeds dried out, young trees were later substituted. Seminoles carried oranges into the Florida wilderness and today, the Seville or sour orange trees thrive deep in the Everglades! Sour oranges grow wild from Jacksonville to Key West. Also, they are grown for grafting, as well as their fruit, which substitutes well for lemons. Seville oranges are part of many wonderful liqueurs. If you find a recipe calling for sour oranges and lack them, mix one part orange juice and one part lemon to replace the ingredient.

Central Florida's citrus industry was devastated by the first of two cold snaps known as the Great Freeze of 1894–1895. And since the late 1940s, orange juice became a breakfast staple after the U.S. Army lead the way in the development of frozen concentrate.

In the nineties orange grove acreage dropped to 791,000 acres, a decrease caused in the 1980s when four severe freezes destroyed many groves in the northern tier of citrus country. During the last 20 years, the industry lost 80 percent of production, according to a spokesperson with the Florida Department of Agriculture and Consumer Services. The culprit is a disease called citrus greening, which began in 2005. In 2004, citrus growers produced 242 million boxes of oranges. In contrast, for the 2021–2022 season, the U.S. Department of Agriculture estimates a production of 42.1 million boxes for Florida. It is close to World War II yields when only 40.87 million boxes were produced in the 1937–1938 era.

Citrus is a big industry in Florida, with more than 375,000 acres devoted to growing oranges, grapefruit, and tangerines. From where it made landfall in southwest Florida in 2022, Hurricane Ian continued to travel over four of the five largest citrus producing counties and brought heavy winds and excessive rainfall that severely damaged the crop.

The largest amusement park in the world and the fun capital of Florida, with 30,500 acres or 47 square miles occupied by the Magic Kingdom, Epcot and MGM Studios, hotels, campgrounds, and nightclubs, Walt Disney World Resorts continues to morph. Yet to come are more thrill rides, exotic landscapes and wildlife areas, as well as various communities of homes. Celebration, Florida, is one example of their master-planned communities.

Central Florida's land is still rich in deer, quail, doves, and other game. Truck lands produce fine beans, snap beans, cabbage, tomatoes, peas, cucumbers, and lettuce. Honey is plentiful, as are poultry and beef, milk and eggs.

Marjorie Kinnan Rawlings, who won a Pulitzer Prize for her much-loved novel *The Yearling* in 1939, lived in a rural settlement called Cross Creek, near Hawthorne, for two decades. The book became an award-winning movie. Her popular cookbook, *Cross Creek Cookery*, published in 1942, celebrates the cooking of the heartland. While the Disney resort hotels, especially the Epcot restaurants, feature international fare, in the heartland homes, traditional Southern food continues as popular as it was a hundred years ago.

Hearts of Palm: A Native Vegetable

The Ocala National Forest is home to our largest population of black bears, though they live everywhere except the Keys. Bears were once hunted for meat, fat, and skins in Florida. Today, they cannot be hunted. As part of their diet, they, like we, enjoy one of our best native vegetables. The white, tender cylindrical heart of the palmetto palm is often referred to as swamp cabbage. Various palms' cores can be eaten. A tree will die after harvesting. As a result, the peach palm or *bactris gasipaes* has been domesticated for harvesting and canning. Hearts of palm are in most grocery stores. They are most often used in cold salads.

Clewiston Fish Fry

Sugar is the big industry in Clewiston, and sweet-meated freshwater catfish from Lake Okeechobee hot from the frying pan, accompanied by crusty hush puppies, are the favorite foods at lakeside barbecues and restaurants.

. . .

Fried Catfish

2 pounds skinned, pan-dressed catfish
1 beaten egg
2 Tbsp. milk
1 cup white cornmeal
2 tsp. salt
Oil for deep frying
Parsley
Lemon slices

Clean and wash catfish. Dry on absorbent paper. Combine egg and milk in one bowl, cornmeal and salt in another. Dip fish into egg mixture then into cornmeal mixture. Heat oil to 350°F and fry fish until golden brown, about 8 minutes. Drain on absorbent paper. Garnish with parsley and lemon. Serve with hot hush puppies. Serves 4.

. . .

Hush Puppies

2 cups cornmeal
1 Tbsp. flour
2 tsp. baking powder
1/2 tsp. salt
1 well-beaten egg
1/4 cup water
1 small onion, chopped fine
Bacon drippings, or oil in which fish was fried

Sift together cornmeal, flour, baking powder, and salt. Mix egg, water, and onion in bowl. Combine with dry ingredients and drop from a spoon into 380°F fat, dipping spoon first into hot fat, then into batter. Fry 6 or more at a time until crisp and golden (about 1 minute), lift with slotted spoon, and drain on paper towels. Serve hot with fish, or cook bite-size and serve as appetizers with beverages. Makes 20.

Old-timers say the name originated around the campfire when hunters tossed the hounds these hot breads to keep them quiet.

. . .

Corn Fritters

1 cup corn, drained
2 slightly beaten eggs
1/3 cup flour
1/2 tsp. baking powder
1 tsp. salt
1/8 tsp. pepper
2 Tbsp. salad oil

Mix corn with slightly beaten eggs. Sift together flour, baking powder, salt, and pepper. Combine corn and flour mixtures. Heat oil medium-hot and drop fritter batter into oil. Fry until brown on bottom, turn and brown other side. Serve hot. Makes about 10. (If so desired, these may be sprinkled with a little confectioners' sugar and served as appetizers.)

Vietnamese

About 7,500 Vietnamese live in Central Florida, and about 83 percent of these in Orange County, according to the U.S. Census. In Orlando, a community that has come to be known as "Little Saigon" is adjacent to the downtown. It is known as the Mills 50 district, as the intersection of Mills Avenue and Highway 50 intersect at its heart.

. . .

Vietnamese Fish Sauce

Courtesy of Chef Hai Vonguyen

1 cup white refined sugar
2 cups warm water
2 Tbsp. white vinegar
1 garlic clove, minced
2 limes, juiced
3 red Thai peppers
1 cup fish sauce

Stir sugar into warm water. Add vinegar. Mince garlic and Thai peppers, and add to water and sugar mixture. Stir the fish sauce and lime juice into the bowl. Sauce can be kept in fridge for a month.

Use the fish sauce to marinate in-bone pork chops overnight, then grill the chops over an open flame. Serve with extra fish sauce, steamed rice, and a simple watercress salad.

. . .

Tomato Basil Pie

Courtesy of Una Kruse

3–4 fresh tomatoes, choose fleshier ones with low seed content, slice thin
10–12 basil leaves, finely chopped
1/2 cup green onions, chopped
1 pre-baked pie crust, 9-inch
1 cup grated cheddar cheese
1 cup grated mozzarella cheese
1/4 cup grated parmesan cheese
1/2 cup mayonnaise
Salt and pepper to taste

Pre-bake the pie crust according to package directions and let cool completely before filling. Meanwhile, put sliced tomatoes in a colander, sprinkle with salt and pepper and toss, then let drain for 20 minutes.

Place the three cheeses in a mixing bowl, add the mayonnaise and stir until combined.

Take the baked crust and placed chopped onions on the bottom followed by the basil leaves. Add the drained tomatoes. Spread these evenly in the pan.

Top with the cheese mixture, spreading dollops around the top of the pie evenly, then smoothing almost to the edges of the pie crust. Protect the edges of the crusts from overcooking by using tin foil around the edges or silicone edge covers.

Bake at 350°F for 30 minutes or until lightly browned. Do not slice while hot. Place the pie on a wire rack until it is warm before cutting.

A classic found on many tables and menus across Florida, this home cook tried it at a local restaurant then went home and experimented with various versions. The one she recreated struck the right notes.

Cuban Bread in 1940s Sanford

Robb's Bakery, established by Fred and Evarae Robb in Sanford in 1940, made Cuban bread. Their loaves were attractive to people at the nearby U.S. Naval Air Station, which was active in 1950 because of the Korean War and the Cold War.

Judy Robb said the pilots would call her father with large orders—30 to 50 loaves of Cuban bread. The pilots—who liked the Robb's bread better than what they found in Cuba— took them to the island as gifts. They were 25 cents a loaf.

Clams Athena

Courtesy of Chef Kim Cash and the Island Hotel, Cedar Key

50 count Cedar Key middle neck clams, washed and rinsed well
4 cups white wine
1 cup fresh diced tomatoes
1/2 cup sliced yellow onions
12 oz. fresh spinach leaves
1 cup sliced mushrooms
1/2 cup quartered artichoke hearts
1 Tbsp. chopped garlic
1 tsp. dried oregano
12 oz. cooked pasta, Angel hair preferred, ready to serve
1/2 cup feta cheese, crumbled

Choose a wide bottom skillet with a matching lid.

Place clams in pan, add wine, oregano, and garlic. Then spread the rest of the vegetables over the clams and steam the clams and vegetables until the clams open.

Serve over pasta and sprinkle with feta cheese.

Serves 2.

Cedar Key Clams

The small island community of Cedar Key, located 50 miles southwest of Gainesville in the Gulf of Mexico, is the state's largest producer of farm-raised clams. Clam farmers use seed-to-table practices. They deliver more than 90 percent of the state's total clam cultivation. The island's surrounding waters retain a high quality for many reasons, including little shoreline development. Also, federal- and state-owned properties in the area are dedicated to conserving and maintaining the natural environments.

Puerto Ricans

A notably large community of Puerto Ricans lives in Central Florida, more specifically in Orange, Osceola, Seminole, and Lake Counties. In 2020, the population was 385,000. Many settled in our state after the devastation of Hurricane Maria in 2017 forced migration, bringing an estimated 50,000. Before that disaster, starting in the 1990s, a New Millennial Migration was underway.

Puerto Rican cooking is distinguished by its *adobo* or marinade or rubs for meats and fish as well as its seasonings. One staple is *culantro* (Eryngium foetidum), also called *recao* or serrated coriander or long coriander. Its flavor is stronger than cilantro's. *Culantrillo* is another popular herb (adiantum capillus veneris) or the Maidenhead fern.

. . .

Rice with Pigeon Peas or Arroz con Gandules

Courtesy Rita Rodriquez

2 cups short grain white rice (washed and rinsed twice)
1 15-oz. can pigeon peas, drained
1 packet sazon Goya seasoning mix
2 leaves culantro or recao. If this herb is not available, substitute Goya's Recaito and Achiote seasoning package for the leaves.
2 Tbsp. tomato sauce
4 Tbsp. *sofrito*
2½ cups warmed chicken broth, more may be needed for grains to open
1 cup of smoked ham or smoked pork chop (or combination) cut into cubes

In a cast iron or aluminum pot, sauté the *sofrito* and Goya seasoning on medium heat. Add the broth and tomato sauce, then the drained pigeon peas. Cook for a minute. Add the meats (if using) and then the rice.

Stir once with a fork. Cover pot with a tight-fitting lid. Cook for 20 minutes on low-medium. Check to see if more broth is needed. If rice looks gummy, do not stir. Put lid back on and wait until rice is firm. If you want crunchy rice on the bottom, after the rice is fully cooked, lower temperature to very low and let the pot sit another 5 minutes.

...

Almojábanas

Courtesy of Ruben Nazario

3 cups milk
5 Tbsp. butter
1 tsp. salt
2 cups rice flour
2 tsp. baking powder
3 eggs
1 cup white cheese (queso blanco del país), which can be substituted in part by Parmesan or Gouda
Vegetable oil

This rice and cheese fritter, of Arabic origin, is popular in Puerto Rico, especially during the Christmas season.

Bring the milk and butter to a boil (scald). Mix the flour and the baking powder. Add the milk. Mix well. Add the eggs, one by one. Mix. (If the paste is too runny, bring it back to the stove and cook on medium heat.) Add the cheese and mix. Fry the paste by spoonful in hot oil in a skillet until golden.

Florida Citrus Recipes

...

Christmas Citrus Compote

4 Florida oranges
1 papaya, fresh or canned
1 pineapple, fresh or canned
2 1/2 cups halved, seedless red and
    green grapes (about 1/2 lb.)
1 cup water
1/4 cup sugar
1 stick cinnamon

This holiday fruit compote is laced with spices and wine.

3 whole cloves
1 cup Marsala wine

Cut 3 strips orange peel from 1 orange, using vegetable peeler; reserve. Peel oranges and cut into crosswise slices. Pare papaya, cut in half lengthwise, and remove seeds; cut into cubes. To prepare pineapple, cut off stem and crown ends. Cut off rind all around, from top to bottom; remove eyes with pointed knife. Cut into quarters lengthwise. Cut away core. Cut remaining meat into fingers about 2 inches long. Combine oranges, papaya, pineapple, and grapes in large bowl. Combine wine, water, sugar, cinnamon stick, cloves, and orange peel in saucepan; stir over medium heat until sugar dissolves. Reduce heat and simmer 5 minutes. Remove spices and orange peel. Cool to lukewarm. Pour syrup over fruit in bowl; cover and refrigerate 6 hours or overnight. Serves 12.

. . .

Orange Garlic Pork Tenderloin from Eastern Cuba

Courtesy of Glenna Veiga

2–3 lbs. pork tenderloin
1 head of garlic, minced
1.5–2 tsp. salt
2 Tbsp. olive oil
1/2 gallon of no-pulp Florida orange juice
Cornstarch, optional

Marinate the tenderloin the night before or at least a good 8 hours before cooking. To marinate the tenderloin, rinse the meat, pat dry, then gently pierce several times throughout with a knife, making small slits. When done, salt the tenderloin covering all sides, and then rub on minced garlic. Cover and refrigerate.

When ready to cook, on the stove, heat the olive oil in a Dutch oven or large pot at medium-high heat. When the oil is ready, gently place the pork tenderloin in, turning it every few minutes to brown and sear on all sides. Once it has browned (not cooked thoroughly), pour the orange juice into the pot. It should be enough to just barely cover the tenderloin. Bring to a boil.

Once the orange juice begins to boil, reduce heat to a slow simmer, and cook uncovered. This allows evaporation. It simmers down to a sauce over time. As the orange juice reduces, turn the tenderloin every 15–20 minutes or so, and baste it, to prevent drying. The orange juice should be sufficiently reduced and the tenderloin cooked after 90 minutes to 2 hours. Check internal temperature of pork tenderloin to make sure. Low heat and slow cooking make for more tender pork.

When the pork is cooked, remove it from the pot, and allow it to rest before slicing. In the meantime, turn up the heat again on the orange juice to reduce it further, or, if you prefer a thicker sauce, you may want to add a half teaspoon or more of cornstarch and keep heating and stirring until desired thickness.

Slice the tenderloin into 1-inch rounds, and pour sauce over the pork. It can be served with white long-grain rice, and a side salad.

Serves 6–8.

This recipe is sure to impress, but what's really impressive is how easy it is make. That's what our stepmother Carmen Rodes Veiga told my sister when she shared this recipe. A native of El Caney in Santiago de Cuba and a busy professional in Miami, Carmen was short on time for cooking. This "cooks itself."

. . .

Fruit Salad with Orange Cream Salad Dressing

1 egg
3 Tbsp. sugar
1/4 tsp. salt
1/4 tsp. ginger
2 tsp. butter
1/2 cup fresh orange juice
11/2 Tbsp. fresh lemon juice
1/4 cup heavy cream, whipped

Fruits for Salad:
Fresh orange sections
Grapefruit sections
Pitted grapes
Pineapple chunks
Crisp salad greens

Beat egg in top of double boiler. Add sugar, salt, ginger, butter, orange juice, and lemon juice; mix well. Place over boiling water and cook, stirring constantly, until mixture thickens slightly, 5 to 7 minutes. Chill. Just before serving, fold in whipped cream. Arrange fresh fruit on crisp greens; serve with dressing. Makes 1 cup of dressing, enough for 6 servings.

. . .

Grapefruit Cole Slaw

2 Florida grapefruit
3 cups shredded cabbage
1¹/₃ cup mayonnaise
¹/₂ tsp. salt
2 tsp. sugar
¹/₂ tsp. celery seed

Chill grapefruit. Cut off peel in strips from top to bottom, slicing deep enough to remove white membrane. Then cut out sections from top to bottom, removing any remaining membrane. Place sections in bowl with cabbage. Combine remaining ingredients; add to cabbage. Toss lightly. Serves 6.

. . .

Baked Stuffed Pork Chops

8 1-inch rib or loin pork chops
Salt, pepper
2 Tbsp. oil
1 cup finely diced celery
1 6-oz. can frozen Florida grapefruit concentrate, thawed and divided
3 cups stale ¹/₄-inch bread cubes
3 Tbsp. minced onion
¹/₄ tsp. salt
¹/₂ tsp. Tabasco
¹/₃ cup brown sugar

Sprinkle pork chops with salt and pepper. Brown in oil in skillet until golden brown on both sides, 15 to 20 minutes. Remove pork chops, saving 4 tablespoons of pan oil. Combine celery, ¹/₄ cup grapefruit juice concentrate, and pan oil; cook over medium heat 2 minutes. Add bread cubes, onion, salt, and Tabasco; mix thoroughly. Combine remaining 1/2 cup grapefruit juice concentrate and brown sugar. Pour over pork chops in casserole. Arrange stuffing on top of pork chops. Bake, covered, in 350°F oven 30 minutes; remove cover and bake 15 minutes longer or until chops are tender. Serves 8.

. . .

Orange Sweet Potato Cups

3 lbs. sweet potatoes
3 Tbsp. melted butter
1/2 cup sugar
1 tsp. salt
1 tsp. vanilla
2 tsp. grated orange rind
1 1/3 cup orange juice
3 Temple or Navel oranges
1 cup mini marshmallows

Boil sweet potatoes until tender; remove skins, mash, and mix with all ingredients except oranges and marshmallows. Cut oranges in half crosswise; remove all juice and pulp but keep rind whole. Fill with hot sweet potato mixture. Place in greased baking pan and bake 30 minutes at 350°F. Garnish with marshmallows and return to oven to brown. Serves 6.

. . .

Grapefruit–Avocado Salad

3 small heads Bibb lettuce
1 large grapefruit, peeled and sectioned
1 medium avocado, sliced lengthwise
1 large purple onion, sliced thin
1 cup pineapple chunks
Tart French dressing

Chill all ingredients. Carefully trim out lettuce core so that the head will sit flat. For each serving, place washed lettuce on a plate and tuck into the leaves grapefruit sections, avocado slices, onion, and pineapple chunks. Serve with tart French dressing. Serves 4.

...

Molasses–Orange Bread

1/2 cup sugar
2 2/3 cups sifted all–purpose flour
1/2 tsp. baking soda
2 tsp. baking powder
1 1/2 tsp. salt
1 cup coarsely chopped pecans
2 1/3 cup evaporated milk
1 Tbsp. grated orange rind
1/2 cup orange juice
2 Tbsp. salad oil
1/2 cup unsulphured molasses

Sift together sugar, flour, baking soda, baking powder, and salt; add nuts. Combine evaporated milk, orange rind, orange juice, salad oil, and molasses. Add to flour mixture all at once; stir just to blend. Turn into a well–greased loaf pan 9 × 5 × 3 inches. Bake in 325°F oven 1 hour 15 minutes. Cool before removing from pan. Makes 1 loaf.

...

Orange Meringue Pie

1/4 cup sugar
1/4 cup cornstarch
1/8 tsp. salt
1 cup orange juice
1/2 cup water
1 Tbsp. lemon juice
3 egg yolks, slightly beaten
1 Tbsp. grated orange rind
1 Tbsp. butter
3 egg whites
1/4 tsp. salt
6 Tbsp. sugar
1 baked 9–inch pie shell

Combine sugar, cornstarch, and salt in medium saucepan; slowly blend in orange juice, water, and lemon juice. Cook and stir over medium heat until mixture is thickened and clear. Slowly stir a little of the hot mixture into egg yolks; add to remaining mixture. Blend in orange rind and butter; mix well. Cool thoroughly. Spoon into cooled pie shell.

Beat egg whites with salt until frothy. Add sugar gradually, beating well after each addition. Continue to beat until stiff peaks form. With a spoon, place mounds of meringue over pie filling, spreading to cover filling completely to edge of crust. Bake in 350°F oven 12 to 15 minutes. Cool thoroughly.

. . .

Orange Pecan Refrigerator Cookies

$1/2$ cup butter
1 cup sugar
$1/4$ tsp. salt
1 tsp. grated orange rind
1 egg, slightly beaten
3 tsp. baking powder
3 cups flour, sifted
$1/4$ cup orange juice
$1^1/2$ cups pecan halves
1 egg white
Sugar, for sprinkling

In one bowl, cream together butter, sugar, and salt until light and fluffy; add orange rind and egg. Beat thoroughly. In another bowl, place baking powder and flour; sift together twice. To the creamed butter mixture add first the flour mixture, then the orange juice in 3 additions, stirring each time until well blended. Roll in wax paper and store in refrigerator overnight to chill thoroughly. Slice thin, keeping any unused dough in refrigerator as cookies bake.

Place slices on an oiled cookie sheet; press a pecan half into the top of each cookie and then brush it with unbeaten egg white. Sprinkle with sugar. Bake in a 375°F oven 10 to 12 minutes, until lightly browned. Cool on racks; store in airtight cookie jar. Makes about 60.

• • •
Orange Juice Cake Surprise

1 large orange
1/2 cup sugar
1 cup raisins
1/4 cup chopped walnuts
1 cup sugar
1/2 cup margarine
2 unbeaten eggs
1 tsp. vanilla
2 cups sifted all-purpose flour
1 tsp. baking soda
1/2 tsp. salt
1/4 cup buttermilk

Squeeze juice from orange; add 1/2 cup sugar, stir, and set aside. Run orange peel and raisins through fine blade of food processor; add nuts and set aside.

Using mixer, beat margarine and add 1 cup sugar, a little at a time. Beat in eggs, one at a time. Add vanilla. Sift together twice the flour, baking soda, and salt; add this alternately with buttermilk in four additions, beating smooth after each. Stir in fruit and walnuts. Turn into greased 9 × 9 × 2 inch pan.

Bake in 350°F oven about 45 minutes. Cool cake in pan 5 minutes, then pour orange juice mixture over it and wait 1 hour before serving warm as pudding, cold as refrigerator cake.

• • •
Feathery Lemon–Cheese Cake

1 cup butter
1 cups sugar
4 eggs
3 cups sifted flour
3 tsp. baking powder
1/2 tsp. salt
1 cup milk
1/2 tsp. vanilla
1/2 tsp. lemon flavoring

The old-fashioned filling in this cake has no cheese in it, but its flavor and texture resemble cheese.

Cream butter and sugar. Add one whole egg at a time, beating after each. Beat about 1 minute after all eggs have been added. Sift together dry ingredients twice. Add dry ingredients to creamed mixture, alternately with milk. Stir in vanilla and lemon flavoring. Grease and flour 3 9-inch round cake pans. Pour batter into pans and bake in 350°F oven 40 minutes or until done. When cool, fill with Lemon-Cheese Filling (see below). Cake may be sprinkled with confectioners' sugar or frosted with Coconut Seven-Minute Frosting (see page 103). Or, a double amount of filling may be made, the whole cake frosted and filled with the lemon-cheese mixture.

Lemon-Cheese Filling
1 cup sugar
4 Tbsp. cornstarch, dissolved in a little water
Juice of 2 lemons
3 Tbsp. butter
2 eggs
2 egg yolks

Combine all ingredients and cook over hot water in double boiler, stirring constantly, until thick. Cool before spreading between layers.

. . .

Meyer Lemon Cake, Curd, and Frosting

Courtesy of Cheryl Kenney

> *A longtime food aficionado who once owned a restaurant and is now a busy caterer, Cheryl Kenney continues exploring various cuisines. Her celebrated backyard Meyer lemon tree bears fruit that enhances many dishes, especially baked goods. She prefers the Meyer lemon as it is not as tart as lemon.*

Cake:

1/2 cup butter, slightly softened
1 1/2 cup sugar
2 cup cake flour or all-purpose flour, sifted twice
4 tsp. canola oil
4 tsp. baking soda

1 tsp. salt
½ cup Bird's Custard Powder
Zest of one Meyer lemon
4 eggs
½ cup milk
½ cup canola oil
½ cup limoncello

Combine first eight ingredients in the bowl of mixer and mix on low until resembles coarse sand. Add eggs and beat until well combined. Add liquids and beat until well combined, scraping sides of bowl.

For an easy cake, pour into well-greased Bundt pan and bake at 350°F for 40–50 minutes until skewer comes out clean. Allow to cool before turning out of pan and glazing with a simple lemon sugar "syrup."

For a special occasion cake, bake in two greased and floured cake pans at 350°F for 25–30 minutes until cake springs back to touch.

Layer cake with Meyer Lemon Curd and Meyer Lemon Butter Cream Frosting.

Meyer Lemon Curd:

½ cup fresh Meyer lemon juice
⅓ cup sugar
Zest from 1 Meyer lemon
2 egg yolks, well beaten
2 eggs, well beaten
Pinch salt
6 Tbsp. unsalted butter in small chunks

Combine all ingredients except butter in bowl over simmering water. Whisk together until warm but not cooking. Add butter and continue whisking until butter melts and is incorporated. Increase heat so that water is at a rolling boil and continue whisking until mixture coats the back of a spoon.

Set aside until ready to assemble cake.

Meyer Lemon Buttercream Frosting:

6 egg whites
1 tsp. cream of tartar
2 cups sugar
2/3 cup water
Zest of 1 Meyer lemon
5 sticks unsalted butter, softened and whipped

Heat sugar, water, and lemon zest over medium-high heat until it comes to a soft boil. In the meantime, beat egg whites and cream of tartar with the whisk attachment in the bowl of mixer until egg whites are firm, slowly drizzle sugar water mixture into the egg whites and once incorporated, turn mixer to high and allow to beat until the bowl is no longer warm to touch. This will take 5–10 minutes. Do not rush the process!

When completely cooled, slowly add whipped butter and mix to utter perfection.

Slice each cake layer in half and fill with Meyer Lemon Curd and then frost with the Meyer Lemon Buttercream for a show-stopping dessert.

. . .

Heavenly Cream Ambrosia

1 cup heavy cream, whipped
1/2 cup sour cream
1 Tbsp. orange liqueur
2 cups orange sections
1 cup grapefruit sections
1 cup freshly grated coconut
1 cup miniature marshmallows

Whip cream then fold in sour cream and orange liqueur. Dice orange sections and grapefruit. Fold into cream with coconut and marshmallows. Cover and chill overnight. Garnish with sliced orange steeped in orange liqueur. Serves 8.

True traditional Southern ambrosia is simply orange sections tossed with freshly grated coconut and a bit of sugar. Marvelous though it is, this recipe is even more so.

Tropicali Punch

1 6-oz. can frozen limeade concentrate
2 6-oz. cans frozen pineapple juice concentrate
1 6-oz. can frozen orange juice concentrate
13 6-oz. cans (9¼ cups) water
2 cups superfine sugar
3 12-oz. bottles cold ginger ale
Maraschino cherries
Fresh orange dices
Mint sprigs

Thaw all concentrates; add sugar and water, stirring until all sugar dissolves. Just before serving, place ice in large punch bowl; pour juices over ice. Add ginger ale, cherries, and orange slices. Serve in glasses with mint sprig. (Orange sherbet may be used in bowl instead of ice, if desired.) Serves 30.

Iced Tea Punch

2 Tbsp. loose tea
2 cups boiling water
1 cup granulated sugar
1 cup orange juice
½ cup lemon juice
12-oz. bottle cold ginger ale

Pour boiling water over tea and let stand 5 minutes. Strain tea into pitcher. Add sugar; stir until dissolved. Pour in juices and chill. To serve, pour over ice in punch bowl and add ginger ale. Makes 10 cups.

Citrus Kiwi Compote

2 oranges, peeled, seeded, sectioned
2 pink grapefruit, peeled, seeded, sectioned
1 8-oz. can pineapple chunks, undrained
4 kiwi fruits, peeled and thinly sliced
2 limes
½ cup apple juice

3 Tbsp. sugar
1/2 gallon orange sherbet

In a large bowl, combine oranges, grapefruit, pineapple, and kiwi fruit. Cut one lime in half. Slice one of the halves thinly and place in bowl with the fruit. Squeeze remaining 1½ limes, strain the juice, and add it to the fruit mixture. Stir in apple juice. Sprinkle with sugar. Cover and refrigerate several hours. Spoon fruit into dessert dishes and top with orange sherbet. Serves 8.

Beef Recipes

...

Tea-Marinated Florida Beef Roast

Brown a 3- to 5-lb. Florida chuck or shoulder cut beef roast in 2 to 3 tablespoons oil. Make enough very strong tea to cover the roast ¼ way. Simmer 3 to 5 hours, until meat is fork tender. Drain off tea and place meat in baking dish. Pour half of the following sauce over the meat. Bake uncovered at 325°F for 45 minutes, basting several times during baking.

Sauce:
1 cup chili sauce
3 Tbsp. brown sugar
Juice of 2 lemons
1 Tbsp. Worcestershire sauce
1/4 tsp. celery salt
1 1/3 cup grated onion
2 Tbsp. bacon drippings
1 cup water
1 tsp. paprika
3 Tbsp. vinegar
1 tsp. salt

Statewide winner in Florida Beef Council contest!

Combine all ingredients and stir to blend. Heat reserved sauce and serve it with the meat.

···

Beef Corn-Pone Pie

1 lb. ground beef
1 20-oz. can tomatoes
1 medium onion, chopped
1 medium green pepper, thinly sliced
3 Tbsp. salad oil
1 20-oz. can kidney beans
Salt to taste
1 tsp. chili powder (or to taste)

Cook onion and pepper in hot oil until onion is transparent but not brown. Add beef; cook until lightly browned. Stir in remaining ingredients; let simmer. Add chili powder just before topping with cornbread mixture.

···

Cornbread

1½ cups cornmeal
3 Tbsp. flour
1 tsp. salt
1 tsp. baking soda
2 cups buttermilk
1 beaten egg
2 Tbsp. bacon drippings, butter, or margarine

Mix and sift dry ingredients. Add buttermilk and egg, stirring until well blended. Heat fat in skillet and add to batter. Turn beef mixture into iron frying pan. Mix batter well, pour over beef mixture, and bake in 450°F oven about 25 minutes, or until golden brown. Serves 6.

In "Culinary Passions" by Antoinette Libro, the poet celebrates
the cooking of various literary women, including Marjorie Kinnan
Rawlings. Three stanzas from her poem follow:

> Another woman of words, Marjorie Kinnan Rawlings
> dearly loved to cook and throw dinner parties,
> serving up alligator-tail steak, cream of peanut soup,
> Minorcan gopher stew and mayhaw jelly.
>
> She filled her Cross Creek Cookery with recipes
> gleaned from remote wilds of north central Florida
> and found her muse deep in the Cracker world of
> people and pine, lore of hammocks and live oaks.
>
> Her "Utterly Deadly Southern Pecan Pie"
> made with heaps of sugar, eggs, crushed pecans
> and Southern cane syrup was, like Emily's
> "Black Cake," an extraordinary concoction.

Printed with permission from *The Marjorie Kinnan Rawlings
Journal of Florida Literature*, volume 29.

. . .

Barbecue Beef Loaf

2 lbs. ground beef
1/4 cup milk
1/4 cup diced onion
2 beaten eggs
1 1/2 cups soft breadcrumbs
2 tsp. salt
1/8 tsp. pepper
1 medium carrot, grated
1/4 cup ketchup
3 Tbsp. brown sugar
2 Tbsp. prepared mustard

Pour milk over breadcrumbs. Add ground beef, salt, pepper, carrot, onion, and beaten eggs. Mix thoroughly. Pack into 5 × 9 inch loaf pan. Mix together ketchup, brown sugar, and mustard, and spread on loaf. Bake in 300°F oven about 1½ hours, or until brown and done. Serves 8.

. . .

Flank Steak Rolls

2 lbs. flank steak, cut in half
1 lb. mild sausage
¼ tsp. basil
½ tsp. thyme
3 Tbsp. bacon drippings
1 28-oz. can tomatoes
1 6-oz. can tomato paste
1 large onion, chopped
3 tsp. salt
¼ tsp. pepper
1½ tsp. chili powder
½ clove garlic
12-oz. package wide noodles
Butter or margarine

Have butcher cut meat to half thickness. Pound steak, sprinkle with basil and thyme, then spread with sausage. Roll and tie with string. Brown in hot drippings; add all remaining ingredients except noodles and butter. Cover: bring to a boil then reduce to simmer and cook slowly 1½ hours, or until meat is tender. Remove garlic. Cook noodles, drain, then place a large wedge of butter in the hot pan and turn noodles in butter until well coated. Remove string from steak roll and slice one inch thick. Serve meat with sauce atop hot noodles. Serves 6 generously.

. . .

Pioneer Pot Roast

¼ lb. salt pork
Salt and pepper
4 lb. chuck roast of beef
1 clove garlic, minced
Flour, for dredging
4 Tbsp. cooking oil
2 sliced onions
1 bay leaf
1 cup boiling water
1 Tbsp. Worcestershire sauce

Slice salt pork thinly and sprinkle with pepper. Slash roast deeply and insert pork slices. Rub roast with garlic and salt; dredge with flour. Heat oil and brown meat well. Place in large heavy pot, place onion and bay leaf on meat, and pour in boiling water and Worcestershire sauce. Bring to boil then reduce to simmer; cover and simmer 3 hours or until meat is tender. Add more water if needed. Serves 8.

Annual Festivals

This is a starter list of food and beverage festivals in the Heartland. Look for annual festival dates for small towns and agricultural areas. You are guaranteed great local fare, along with entertainment for all generations:

Palatka Blue Crab Festival, the Palatka Craft Beer Festival, the Crescent City Catfish Festival, the Bostwick Blueberry Festival, the Hastings Potato and Cabbage Festival, and the Armstrong Gullah Geechee Festival.

. . .

Mom's Swiss Steak

1½ lbs. round steak, 1½ inches thick
1 tsp. salt
¼ tsp. pepper
¼ cup flour
2 Tbsp. cooking oil
1 clove garlic, minced
2 large onions, sliced
1 Tbsp. Worcestershire sauce
2 8-oz. cans tomato sauce
1 dash red hot sauce

Trim fat edges from meat. Combine salt, pepper, and flour. Divide in half and pound half of mixture into each side of steak. Heat oil in heavy frying pan and brown meat quickly on both sides. Add remaining ingredients, cover, reduce to simmer, and cook about 2 hours or until meat is tender. If desired, thicken sauce before serving with meat. Serves 6.

. . .

Golden Onion Gravy for Steak

4 cups sliced onions
2 Tbsp. cooking oil
2 Tbsp. flour
2 cups meat stock
1 Tbsp. Worcestershire sauce
Salt
Freshly ground pepper

Heat oil in heavy frying pan and cook onions until light golden brown. Gradually stir in flour, stirring until smooth. Add remaining ingredients; reduce heat very low and cook until thick, stirring constantly. Cover and simmer 10 minutes. Serves 6.

. . .

Barbecued Short Ribs

Using 3 pounds beef short ribs, cut meat from bones into serving pieces. Marinate overnight in Southern Barbecue Sauce Supreme or your favorite sauce. Grill over hot charcoal, brushing often with barbecue sauce and turning to brown. Serves 6.

...

Southern Barbecue Sauce Supreme

1 lb. butter
1 pint apple cider vinegar
1 cup water
1 Tbsp. dry mustard
1 large onion, grated
5 Tbsp. Worcestershire sauce
2 cups tomato ketchup
1 cup chili sauce
Juice of 2 lemons
1/2 lemon, left whole, seeded
2 cloves garlic, chopped and tied in cheesecloth bag
1 tsp. sugar
1 bay leaf

Place all ingredients in saucepan and bring to a boil. Reduce to slow heat; simmer 30 minutes, stirring occasionally. Enough for 10 lbs. of beef, lamb, or pork. Keep it warm and when meat on barbecue pit is 1/4 done, swab with sauce frequently until done.

...

Spanish Beefburgers

1/2 cup finely chopped onions
1/4 cup chopped celery
1/4 cup chopped green pepper
3 Tbsp. melted butter
1 can condensed tomato soup
2 Tbsp. Worcestershire sauce
2 Tbsp. vinegar
1 Tbsp. prepared mustard
1 lb. ground beef, shaped into patties
Bacon drippings

Cook onions, celery, and green pepper in butter until onions are transparent. Add all remaining ingredients except beef; mix well and simmer 10 minutes, stirring several times. In frying pan, brown beef patties in bacon drippings and cook until done. Place each patty on toasted roll, pour hot Spanish sauce over, and serve hot. Serves 4 or 5.

...

Scrambled Hot Dogs

6 frankfurters, finely chopped
1/2 cup (2 oz.) shredded cheddar cheese
1 Tbsp. chopped onion
2 Tbsp. chopped sweet pickle
3 Tbsp. ketchup
1 tsp. prepared mustard
2 Tbsp. vegetable oil
1/2 tsp. salt
6 hot dog buns, split

Kids love this one!

Combine frankfurters, cheese, onion, and pickle, stirring well. Mix together ketchup, mustard, oil, and salt; pour this mixture over frankfurter mixture and toss lightly. Spoon mixture into hot dog buns. Wrap each in aluminum foil and bake in 350°F oven for 20 minutes or until heated through. Makes 6 sandwiches.

Mexican Recipes

...

Mexican Shrimp

24 large shrimp
1/2 cup lime juice
1/2 cup olive oil
5 cloves garlic, chopped
3 green chilies, peeled and chopped (or 1/2 tsp. cayenne pepper)
3 Tbsp. melted butter or margarine
Minced parsley

Shell and devein shrimp, leaving tails intact. Marinate overnight in lime juice, oil, and seasonings, using a glass or stainless steel dish. Heat broiler. Remove shrimp from marinade. Place in broiler pan and brush on butter or margarine. Broil until shrimp turns pink, about 3 to 5 minutes. Serve at once, sprinkled with minced parsley. Serves 4–6.

Great appetizers!

Grilled Catfish with Salsa

4 farm-raised catfish fillets or steaks
1/4 tsp. white pepper
1/2 tsp. garlic salt

Salsa
2 large, ripe tomatoes
1 clove garlic, peeled
Green onions, chopped
1 4-oz. can green chiles, chopped
1 tsp. olive oil
1 Tbsp. lime juice
Salt and pepper to taste
Cilantro or parsley to taste (dried or chopped fresh)

Two hours before serving, combine peeled, seeded, quartered tomatoes with garlic, green onions, and green chiles. Coarsely chop in food processor or blender. Stir in olive oil and lime juice. Add salt, pepper, and cilantro to taste. Set aside to stand at least 1 hour for flavors to blend.

Sprinkle fillets with pepper and garlic salt. Place fillets in well-greased fish-grilling basket over hot coals. Grill 10 minutes per inch of thickness, turning once, until fish flakes easily. Serve hot with salsa. Serves 4. (Note: Commercially prepared salsa may be used.)

Pico de Gallo

Courtesy of Marisella Veiga

1 tomato, diced
1 small yellow onion, chopped
5 cilantro sprigs, chopped
1 jalapeño, seeded or not, minced
1/2 lemon's juice
Salt and pepper to taste

Combine the vegetables in a bowl. Squeeze the lemon over it, add salt and pepper, and toss. Refrigerate until time to serve.

. . .

Mexican Rice

1/2 small yellow onion, chopped
1 jalapeño pepper, seeded or not, chopped
1 large tomato or 1/2 can tomato sauce
1 cup white rice, long grain
1 Tbsp. corn oil
12 sprigs or more fresh cilantro
2 cups water or chicken broth or combination
1/4 tsp. cumin seed, ground
1/4 tsp. chili powder
1/8 tsp. ground coriander
Salt and pepper to taste

Heat the oil in a non-stick skillet on medium heat. Toss in unwashed rice, onion, and jalapeño. Let these cook together, moving the rice around on a regular basis until the grains begin to look opaque and then a little toasted, about 9 minutes. You are cooking the rice before it goes into a steaming phase.

When the grains look a little beige, add 2 cups water or chicken broth or combination of both liquids. Then add the tomatoes, stir. Add the seasonings. Bring these to a boil then lower the heat to near simmer. The rice can cook uncovered, but I like to use a lid to cover the skillet for the next 10 minutes of cooking. If there's still liquid in the skillet at this point, take lid off and move the grains so it finally evaporates. Add chopped cilantro at the end.

Serves 4–6.

···

Huevos Rancheros with Tomatillo Salsa

Courtesy of Reynaldo Guerrero

8 or 9 medium tomatillos (husked and washed)
1/2 medium onion
1 jalapeño pepper and 1 serrano pepper (stems removed)

Put these in a pot and cover with water. Bring to a boil, then reduce heat to medium low. Simmer for about 10 minutes or until tomatillos are soft. Save this water.

Place the cooked vegetables in a blender. Add 10–15 sprigs fresh cilantro. Add salt to taste. Ground cumin is optional but 1/4 to 1/2 teaspoon adds flavor.

Then, add some cooking water to the blender so it rises to a little less than half the mixture. Puree until smooth. Add more water if you like a thinner salsa.

Cook eggs over easy and plate them. Cover with salsa. Accompany with warm corn or flour tortillas.

While a red sauce is more common, the Mexican classic is also delicious with a green sauce—this home cook's personal favorite. This dish is welcomed at any meal.

···

Nifty Nachos

12 corn tortillas
Peanut oil
1/2 lb. grated Longhorn cheese
1 can pickled jalapeño slices

Stack the tortillas on a cutting board and cut into 3 wedge-shaped pieces, for 36 pieces total. Heat 1/2 inch of peanut oil in a heavy skillet to 375°F. Fry 4 or 5 tortilla pieces in skillet at a time. Use a spatula to mash them down when they puff up; continue turning and mashing until they are flat, 60 seconds or less. Place cooked tortillas on a paper towel to drain. Drain oil from skillet.

Place crisp tortillas on a microwave-safe platter; cover with grated cheese and jalapeño slices. Microwave on high until cheese melts. Serves 6–8.

Seminole Indians

The pride of the Seminole people, shown in this woman's face, led them to fight for their right to Florida lands.

Think of the Everglades and you think of Seminole Indians, yet they are not natives of Florida! When the Spanish first set foot in northeast Florida, they found Timucuan-speakers who numbered about 150,000, according to historian Jerald T. Milanich. The names of nearly 100 individual Indian groups from that time are known, he writes. The Calusas were fishermen and mariners in southwest Florida who violently opposed the white man's advance, and the Apalachee of the northwest, great farmers and powerful with a strong league of united chiefs. In *Finding Florida*, T. D. Allman writes about First Floridians before European contact. He cites a conservative estimate given by Dr. Henry F. Dobyns: that the peninsula's native inhabitants numbered approximately 925,000.

After the English-Spanish struggle caused by the settling of Georgia and the Carolinas resulted in an English victory and James E. Oglethorpe founded Savannah in 1733, he swept south into Florida. A disastrous war had recently wiped out most of Florida's natives and allies from the Lower Creek tribes came with Oglethorpe to help him fight. They liked the land and decided to stay.

Other Lower Creeks settled in the Apalachee region or moved into other north Florida areas. About 1775, their name became Seminole, which comes from the Spanish word "cimarron" meaning runaway. By 1835, they were firmly settled.

The pride of the Seminole people led them to fight for their right to Florida lands and determination not to move. The seven towns they had in 1799 rapidly increased to 20 or more.

Hostilities with the United States began while the Spanish were still in control, especially during the War of 1812 and again in 1817–1818, now called the first Seminole War. Gen. Andrew Jackson quelled the latter with 3,000 men—one reason for Spain ceding the territory to the United States in 1819.

By the Treaty of Moultrie Creek in 1823, the Seminole ceded most of their lands except a central Florida reservation of four million acres. But pressure continued for their complete removal, so another treaty was negotiated at Payne's Landing in 1832, which compelled them to move west of the Mississippi within three years. This treaty resulted from the Indian Removal Act passed by U.S. Congress in 1830.

Most of the tribe, under Osceola's leadership, repudiated this last treaty, and so began the second war in 1835. It ended in August 1842, and most of the tribe was moved west. But the war was long and the cost was great—1,466 American lives, countless Seminole lives, and $20,000,000. They have never signed a peace treaty or surrendered.

Some 300 Seminoles escaped into the watery wilderness of the Everglades, a slow-moving freshwater river 50 miles wide and a few inches deep, fed by Lake Okeechobee. In 1957, they officially became the Seminole Tribe of Florida. Today they have six reservations: Hollywood, Big Cypress (the largest), Brighton, Immokalee, Fort Pierce, and Tampa. As of September 2022, the total population on the reservations is 4,361, according to the Seminole Tribe of Florida.

Until 1960, most Seminoles lived in "chickees"—a shelter without walls made with four poles, wooden floor, and palm-thatched roof. They differed from their original log homes, and designed in response to a need for quick, disposable shelter. Non-natives have found them useful and attractive; as a result, building chickees has become a lucrative business today. Until millions of new residents cut severely into the hunting and fishing that was the food source for the tribe, the Indians lived a peaceable life among the animals and birds of the Everglades. They had three reservations, in Glades County, Broward County, and Hendry County. However, in 1957 they organized under a federal charter, with more becoming cattle ranchers and operators of successful arts and crafts centers as well as casinos and hotels. The Seminole Okalee Indian Village (open to tourists) is in Hollywood across from their Hollywood Classic Casino. It hosts exhibits from the Ah-Tah-Thi-ki Museum and features a Village and Culture camp with lush landscapes and meeting spaces under traditional chickees.

The Cow Creek Seminoles learned to live and cooperate with the European descendants, although many have not fully accepted them. The Miccosukee, many of whom live along Tamiami Trail and operate restaurants and tourist attractions like the Miccosukee Resort and Gaming as well as the Miccosukee Indian Village, were once more antagonistic and less prosperous. They are culturally Seminoles but in 1962, they organized as the Miccosukee Tribe of Indians of Florida. About 550 are members. Their reservation has three sections: the Alligator Alley Reservation, the Tamiami Trail Reservation, and the Krome Avenue Reservation.

The Seminoles are a proud race, self-reliant, tenacious of their opinions, true to their traditions, with life based on matrilineal lineage. So, a camp is usually composed of a woman, her daughters, and their children, and the husbands and unmarried brothers of these. When a man marries, he goes to his wife's camp, builds her a house, and moves in at one point in time. Each household contained the all-important sewing machine used to make the rainbow-colored, long-skirted costumes of the women and the shirts and jackets of the men. Young and older Seminoles now wear modern dress, but traditional clothing is often still worn by elders.

In their new homes, the Seminoles have modern appliances. At times cooking is still done the old, primitive way deep in the reservations. The campfire is unique. Several logs are arranged like spokes of a wheel, with the fire at the hub. Ends of the long logs extend into the fire and are continually pushed over the flame as it burns the wood.

Over this fire hangs a black iron pot filled with Soffkee, the standby food. This is a stew of meat, usually venison, with meal, grits, and vegetables added. A wooden spoon is used and anyone may dip out a spoonful of stew when hungry, any time of day.

Their fruits are guavas, sour oranges, limes, bananas, wild berries, and plums. In cleared land on the hammocks, Seminoles grow corn, pumpkins, melons, sweet potatoes, and sugar cane. Tender buds of the palmetto (called hearts of palm by the non-indigenous) are eaten year-round, raw or cooked.

When hunting is good, the men bag deer, quail, wild turkey, opossum, rabbit, and squirrel; from Florida waters they take fish, turtles, and oysters. When hunting is poor, they eat the chickens and pigs raised at home.

Coontie is the staff of life, the equivalent of our wheat bread. This wild root grows only in South Florida and is called "God's gift to the Seminole." Very nutritious, it tastes something like arrowroot.

The Seminoles mash this root to pulp in mortars cut into cypress logs called coontie logs. The starch is then separated from the pulp with a straining cloth, yielding a yellowish-white flour used to bake their bright orange bread. At one time, coontie starch was used in food and for laundry, and coontie-making was quite an industry in South Florida.

The Seminoles are successful in tourism, especially hotels and gaming, and in the cattle industry. Florida's status as an important cattle state is so because the Seminoles have played and continue to play key roles. What is more, their history, arts, and culture are highlighted at the Smithsonian-affiliated Ah-Tah-Shi-Ki Museum on the Big Cypress reservation south of Clewiston.

Several chiefs of the tribe have served as Baptist ministers, and many of the Indians have become Christians. Today, they enjoy modern living, give their children good educations, but never surrender revered Indian traditions.

...

Skillet Orange Duck

1/3 cup all-purpose flour
1 1/2 tsp. salt
1/4 tsp. pepper
3 ducks, quartered
1/3 cup butter
1 1/2 cups water
1/3 cup cooking sherry
1/3 cup orange juice
2 Tbsp. orange marmalade
1 Tbsp. grated orange rind

Tip: Rubbing a wild duck with lemon will help kill the gamey taste.

In bag, combine flour, salt, pepper.
Shake duck in bag. Over medium heat in heavy iron skillet, brown duck in butter. Combine all remaining ingredients and pour over duck. Cover; simmer 1 1/2 hours or until tender. Serves 6.

...

Venison Soup

1 3-lb. venison roast
4 cups cold water
1 Tbsp. salt
1 1/2 quarts water
1 bunch celery hearts, sliced
2 cups tomatoes
3 medium potatoes, cubed
4 onions, cubed
1 clove garlic, chopped fine
1 bay leaf
1 Tbsp. parsley
Salt and pepper
Flour, for thickening

Soak roast in cold salt water overnight. Discard water and put meat in 1 1/2 quarts water. Simmer for 2 1/2 hours; remove and cool meat. Place in refrigerator overnight. Next day, skim off fat, simmer 2 hours; 20 minutes before meat is done, add celery, tomatoes, potatoes, onions, garlic, and bay leaf. Add parsley and season to taste with salt and pepper. If necessary, thicken with a little flour. Serves 6–8.

• • •
Oyster–Cornbread Stuffing
for Wild Turkey

6 Tbsp. butter
¼ cup minced onion
4 cups crumbled cornbread
2 lightly beaten eggs
1 pint oysters with liquid
¼ tsp. salt
¼ tsp. paprika
2 Tbsp. minced parsley

Melt butter and sauté onion until golden brown. Stir in all remaining ingredients. Toss lightly to mix. Cool before stuffing bird.

• • •
Fried Green Tomatoes

Use three mature, firm green tomatoes. Wash, dry, and cut in thick slices. Sprinkle with salt, let stand 5 minutes, then drain. Sprinkle with freshly ground black pepper. Dredge in cornmeal and fry in hot oil until lightly browned.

Serve hot. Serves 4.

• • •
Boiled Hard–Shell Crabs

Using 12 live hard–shell crabs, plunge into boiling salted water in heavy large pot, cover and boil 15 to 20 minutes, or until red. Serve on heated platter with cracking tools and individual dishes of melted butter for each person.

Crack shells and pick out the meat on underside of the shell and from the claws, also the tamale or green liver.

. . .

Corn Hoecake

Combine 2 cups white cornmeal with 1 teaspoon salt. Add enough boiling water (it must be boiling hot) to make a medium batter. Let stand for 1 hour. Heat bacon drippings in a heavy frying pan and place a heaping tablespoon full of batter in hot pan. Press down lightly with spatula to make cakes ¹/₂-inch thick. When one side is golden brown, turn and brown the other. Serve very hot. Especially good with turnip greens. Serves 6–8.

. . .

Roasting Ears

Using 4 ears unhusked fresh sweet corn, remove outer husks and silks. Leave inner husks on corn. In deep pot, submerge corn in 4 quarts of water with 6 tablespoons salt. Weight corn to hold it under water and soak 1 hour. Remove corn from water, place 1 teaspoon butter inside the ear on the kernels, wrap in aluminum foil, and roast in 450°F oven about 25 minutes or until done. Serve hot with dish of melted butter, plenty of salt and pepper. Serves 4. (Note: Corn may also be roasted amid hot coals in barbecue pit—have coals well burned down with no flames—and cook about 10 minutes.)

. . .

Black-Eyed Peas with Dumplings

1 cup dried black-eyed peas
1 cup water and 1 tsp. salt

Dumplings:
2 cups flour
4 tsp. baking powder
1 tsp. salt
2 oz. salt pork or with peas, not under dumplings
1 Tbsp. cooking oil next to salt pork and under peas
About 1 cup milk

Wash peas, cover with 3 cups water, and soak overnight. Add salt and meat or oil to peas; bring to boil then reduce to simmer and cook covered until beans are tender; 15 minutes before end of cooking time, remove cover. Sift dry ingredients together, then add enough milk to make dough. If necessary, add enough water to peas to make about 1 cup liquid in pot. With fork and spoon, drop walnut-sized bits into peas, cover pot tightly; steam 15 minutes. Serves 4.

· · ·

Baked Pumpkin Bread

1/2 cups sifted flour
1 1/4 tsp. baking soda
1 tsp. salt
1 tsp. ground cinnamon
1/2 tsp. ground nutmeg
1 cup mashed pumpkin
1 cup sugar
1/2 cup buttermilk
1 egg, slightly beaten
2 Tbsp. soft butter

Sift together twice flour, baking soda, salt, and spices. In large bowl, mix well pumpkin, sugar, buttermilk, and slightly beaten egg. Stir in dry ingredients and butter. Beat at medium speed until blended. Turn into greased loaf pan and bake at 350°F for 1 hour.

The Seminoles use cooked, mashed pumpkin mixed with self-rising flour and water to make a soft dough. They knead it in a ball until it is elastic then continue turning and folding until it is about 1/4-inch thick. Small cakes are placed in a heavy iron skillet filled with smoking grease and fried until golden brown on each side. This makes a puffy, crisp bread.

This contemporary version of traditional bread is made with pumpkin but is baked in the oven!

· · ·

Fried Frogs' Legs

Soak frogs' legs in equal amounts of salt water and milk for 1 hour. Drain, pat dry. Shake in bag of seasoned flour. Sauté in hot oil or butter until tender and brown. Serve with lemon or lime wedges.

...
Baked Rabbit

Skin and dress rabbit and cut into serving pieces. Shake in a bag of flour seasoned with salt and pepper. Fry in butter or bacon drippings until golden brown. Place in baking dish; cover with milk. Bake in 350°F oven about 1 hour or until tender. Mix a little flour with water and use to thicken milk for gravy. Pour over rabbit; serve hot.

Hoecakes Are Here!

"Hoecakes were made by pouring cornmeal onto the blade of a long-handled hoe and baking it over hot cinders. The hoe was brought to the Americas by West and Central African farmers during the Atlantic Slave trade."
Fred Ople in *Zora Neale Hurston on Florida Food: Recipes, Remedies and Simple Pleasures.*

Suwannee River Country

*After Tallahassee was named territorial government seat,
lawmakers met in this three-story Capitol building.*

From Tallahassee to Gainesville, time has not touched the fairy-tale beauty of the gently rolling red clay hills, azure lakes, and great live oaks trailing Spanish moss. The Suwannee River meanders lazily between banks of lush green and shadowed by the spreading arms of ancient trees across the state from its birthplace in the Okefenokee Swamp in southeast Georgia. Its tannic-colored waters, created by decaying vegetation, move to the Gulf. The Stephen Foster Folk Cultural Center State Park on its banks in White Springs has hosted an annual folk festival since 1953. The three-day festival on Memorial Day weekend celebrates Florida's traditional arts—culinary included.

To the north and west, almost in the center of the panhandle, lies Tallahassee, a Creek Indian word meaning "Old Town." The north Florida area was first explored by Panfilo de Narvaez who landed at Tampa Bay in February 1528. In May, he led an overland expedition with the hope of subduing natives and colonizing Florida and beyond. It ended in July in St. Marks, near the mouth of the St. Marks River. So fierce was the native opposition to his march that only four men made it to Mexico to tell of the failed expedition.

St. Marks eventually became an important port to the Spanish missions. Fort San Marcos de Apalache was built in 1679 by the Spanish. It was later occupied by the English, then American, then Confederate forces.

In 1539, Navaez was followed by Hernando de Soto who landed in the Tampa Bay area and took his men north into Georgia, fighting Indians all the way past an Indian village near the modern city of Ocala, and into Tallahassee.

The city's first item of recorded history is dated 1539, when de Soto held a meeting with the controlling Apalachee tribes, but this must have been a center for Indian activity long before that. De Soto wintered near Tallahassee with a 600-man party, and it is believed that this marked the first observance of Christmas in the New World.

In the seventeenth century, Spanish missions were strung out on the Suwannee and throughout north Florida from St. Augustine to the Gulf. One of these was the Apalachee-Spanish-Franciscan Mission of San Luis, established in 1656 near Tallahassee. It was evacuated and destroyed in 1704. Today it is a beautiful living history museum whose workers demonstrate many old culinary traditions including the native creation of barbacoa, our early barbeque. The mission has a YouTube video on making hard tack or galletas. The Friary's kitchen included hickory nuts to make ink and milk, mustard seeds and mint for digestive problems.

The Apalachee lived on fertile land once called the Apalachee Province of Anhaica. Great farmers with extensive cultivation, they supplied foods to the mission and also exported food to St. Augustine and to Havana.

A larger Old World learned of the beauty of the Suwannee River country with its springs and underground caverns when, just after the Revolutionary War in 1791, famous travel writer and botanist William Bartram published a book describing his Florida travels. *The Travels of William Bartram* is still in print, and the book recreated the beauty of the region. Some scholars believe it inspired many lines in Coleridge's poem "Kubla Khan."

Our northern neighbor, Georgia, is another example of how geography plays a key role in cultural fusion. In 1732, Georgia was the last of the British colonies to be established. Founder James Oglethorpe designed it as a Debtor's Colony. Slavery was banned yet this changed by Royal Decree in 1751.

The colony protected South Carolina and the other colonies from Spanish invasion potentially coming from what was then Spanish Florida.

In February 1763, the First Treaty of Paris brought a big change: Spain gave Britain all of Florida in exchange for Cuba and the Philippines. The British ruled Florida from 1763 to 1784. When this transpired, most of the Spaniards in St. Augustine, along with many Africans and Timucuans, moved to Cuba.

In 1812, Georgia settlers established a Republic of Florida. They were tormented by repeated Indian raids from tribes to the south until General Andrew Jackson swept down into Florida in 1814 to do battle. A Spanish fort on the St. Marks River called San Marcos de Apalache was seized by Andrew Jackson in 1818 during the First Seminole War. His victories weakened the hold of Spain on Florida cities, forcing the Spanish to sell Florida to the United States for five million dollars in the Adams–Onis Treaty of 1819.

On March 4, 1824, Tallahassee came into its own, when it was named the capital of the American Territory of Florida. A log cabin was its first state capitol building. During its first half century, the city saw rowdy backwoodsmen mingling on the streets with wealthy planters from Georgia, North Carolina, and Virginia.

Social life was lively and festive, led by such celebrities as Prince Achille Murat, nephew of Napoleon Bonaparte. The prince bought a large plantation to grow cotton, calling it Lipona near Tallahassee. In 1826, he married Catherine Willis, great-grandniece of George Washington, in Tallahassee. He recorded details of the elaborate dinner parties in his journal, writing, "No news in town except a wine party, or rather eating, drinking, card playing and see-gar smoking."

The burial place of the prince and his lady is in the Old St. John's Episcopal Church Cemetery, one of the town sights.

The longest and costliest of U.S. Indian wars raged from 1835 to 1842, finally forcing the Seminoles to abandon their beloved hill country and to flee south for safety into the Everglades.

The inflow of settlers increased and by 1845, there were many great plantations in north Florida raising cotton and sugar cane, producing cattle and hogs. The pretentious Maryland and Virginia late Georgian Colonial mansions built then still stand, giving the area a genuine aura of the Old South. Less elaborate but equally well-proportioned are at least a dozen more mansions built in the 1830s in the antebellum towns of Madison, Monticello, Quincy, and Marianna.

The farming town of Quincy, northwest of Tallahassee, was once the wealthiest town per capita in the United States. At least 67 of its residents became known as Coca-Cola millionaires, thanks to a local banker urging people to buy shares in the company while they were cheap during the Great Depression.

South Florida's boom skipped past this part of the state, so the natural beauty remains largely intact. What began as a 15-home settlement is now a busy city with close to 200,000 residents. Yet Tallahassee has not succumbed to the cosmopolitanism of a tourist state.

One still finds stately, white-columned homes furnished with rare antiques. Magnificent gardens are aflame with camellia, japonica, and azalea each spring. Civil War trenches and breastworks adorn the town park.

Downtown, a modern 22-story State Capitol, designed by award-winning architect Edward Durell Stone, was built in 1977 and stands alongside the smaller historic Capitol building, completed in 1845. It offers visitors exhibits of Florida history.

Since 1857, Tallahassee has been the home to Florida State University; since 1887, it has been home to Florida Agricultural and Mechanical University. Today, its combined college student population is more than 70,000.

In this placid land of magnolias and oleanders, the mint julep is popular and Southern food reigns. From nearby farmlands come garden vegetables, sweet potatoes, watermelons, pecans, corn, peanuts, Irish potatoes, and sugar cane.

Game birds, homegrown beef, hogs, and chickens are plentiful. Fried chicken, cornbread and biscuits, fruit puddings and pies, rich milk and cream desserts—these are among the homemade dishes still served with warm hospitality in north Florida homes.

. . .

Tallahassee Rice

Courtesy of Carolyn Smith

1 cup white rice
1 stick butter
2 cans beef consommé soup
1 yellow onion, chopped

In a skillet, sauté the onion in the butter until soft. Add rice and stir with a wooden spoon. Add both cans of soup. Bake in covered casserole for an hour at 350°F. Variation: Instead of fresh onion, substitute a can of onion soup for one can of consommé.

The simple yet flavorful rice dish is named for our state capital and has also traveled to surrounding areas. This classic recipe was made regularly in the home of Katie Cannon Smith and was shared by her daughter. The Smiths were farmers in nearby Quincy, Florida.

. . .

Chicken Mousse

2 envelopes gelatin
1/2 cup cold water
1/2 cup boiling chicken stock
1 cup cool stock
1 tsp. Worcestershire sauce
Salt and pepper to taste
2 cups diced white chicken meat
1 cup diced celery
1/2 cup mayonnaise
1/2 cup heavy cream, whipped

North Florida folk sometimes serve this with chilled watermelon rind pickles.

½ cup grated almonds
2 tsp. chopped parsley

Soften gelatin in cold water. Stir into hot stock until dissolved then combine with cool stock, Worcestershire sauce, salt, and pepper. Refrigerate until consistency is like honey. Add all remaining ingredients. Turn into oiled mold. Chill until set then unmold and garnish with parsley. Serves 6.

...

Green Bean Salad

3 cups cooked green beans, drained
2 cups cooked green peas, drained
¼ cup stuffed olives, sliced
¼ cup almonds, sliced
2 cups celery, cut in ½-inch strips
1 cup green onions, sliced
2 cups raw carrots, cut in ½-inch strips
1 bottle French salad dressing
2 slices bacon, cooked, drained, and crumbled

Combine ingredients except bacon and marinate overnight in French dressing. Drain before serving. Crumble bacon over top just before serving. Serves 20.

...

Willie's Chicken Dressing

Chicken giblets
1 tsp. salt
4 peppercorns
1 onion, stuck with 4 cloves
1 carrot, scraped
3 cups crumbled cornbread
3 cups crumbled biscuits
1 tsp. salt
1 tsp. poultry seasoning
2 medium onions, chopped fine
3 celery stalks, chopped fine
1 cup pecans, chopped fine

Guests frequently skip the chicken to save room for this superb dressing.

The night before, place chicken giblets in 1 quart of salted water with peppercorns, onion, and carrot; bring to a boil and reduce heat to simmer to make chicken stock. Set aside giblets to use in gravy. Mix together all ingredients; add enough stock to moisten. Pack into square, greased baking pan and bake in 350°F oven until brown, 25–30 minutes. Dressing may also be used to stuff the bird instead of being baked separately. Serves 6–8.

. . .

Chicken Giblet Gravy

Chicken giblets and neck
4 peppercorns
1 onion, stuck with 4 cloves
1 carrot, scraped
3 Tbsp. flour
1 hard-cooked egg, chopped
Salt and pepper

If giblets have not been cooked (as in above recipe), place giblets in 1 quart of water with salt, peppercorns, onion, and carrot; bring to boil then reduce heat to simmer. Cook until tender. Chop giblets and neck meat and set aside. Strain broth, discarding vegetables. Remove chicken from roasting pan; pour out all but 3 tablespoons drippings. Over low heat, blend in flour, stirring constantly. Pour 1 cup giblet broth into roasting pan and stir until brown bits are loose. Add remaining 1 cup of broth and stir until gravy is very smooth and hot. Add chopped giblets and chopped, hard-cooked egg. Correct seasoning. Makes 2 cups.

. . .

Cheesy Squash Casserole

Courtesy of Louise Brown Dunnavan

2 lbs. yellow squash
1 lb. zucchini squash
1/2 cup chopped onion
1 Tbsp. sugar
1/2 tsp. salt
Dash of black pepper
1 cup water

4 slices crisp bacon, crumbled
1 cup grated cheddar cheese
1/4 tsp. marjoram
1 well-beaten egg
1 cup buttered breadcrumbs

Born and raised in Lee, Madison County, Florida, Louise Brown Dunnavan shares a family recipe made with fresh vegetables from the garden, always plentiful!

Slice squash and place in a large saucepan with the chopped onion. Add sugar, salt, pepper, and water. Cover and bring to a boil. Reduce and let simmer 20 minutes or until the squash is tender. Drain and mash with the egg, bacon, cheese, and marjoram and mix well. Spoon the squash mixture into a 2-quart casserole leveling across the top.

Sprinkle top with buttered breadcrumbs. Bake for 25– 30 minutes at 350°F. Serves 6.

Peaches!

Peaches were among the crops brought by the Spanish and eventually grown and traded by the Apalachee. In fact, according to the Mission San Luis, "In North Central Georgia, peaches became the second most common plant grown in the mid-17th century, just behind corn! By the time the English arrived at Jamestown, Virginia in 1607, the natives there were growing peaches."

. . .

Southern Peach Cobbler

Courtesy of Louise Brown Dunnavan

8 fresh peaches, peeled, pitted, and sliced in thin wedges
1/4 cup white sugar
1/4 cup brown sugar
1/4 tsp. ground cinnamon
1/8 tsp ground nutmeg
1 tsp. fresh lemon juice
3 tsp. cornstarch

Biscuit Topping
Mix Together:
1 cup all-purpose flour
3 Tbsp. white sugar
1/4 cup white sugar
1 tsp. ground cinnamon
1/4 cup brown sugar
1 tsp. baking powder
1/2 tsp. salt
6 tbsp. unsalted butter, chilled and cut into small pieces
1/4 cup boiling water

Preheat oven to 425°F.

In a large bowl, combine peaches, 1/4 cup white sugar, 1/4 cup brown sugar, 1/4 teaspoon cinnamon, nutmeg, lemon juice, and cornstarch. Toss to coat evenly and pour into a 2-quart baking dish. Bake in preheated oven for 10 minutes.

Meanwhile, in a large bowl, combine flour, 1/4 cup white sugar, 1/4 cup brown sugar, baking powder, and salt. Blend in butter with a pastry blender until the mixture resembles coarse meal. Stir in water until just combined.

Remove peaches from oven, and drop spoonfuls of topping over them. Sprinkle with the sugar and cinnamon mixture. Bake until topping is golden, about 30 minutes.

Fruit cobblers were a favorite summertime dessert for the Brown family. Louise's mother used whatever fresh fruits were in season to make them. When her father went to Georgia to buy farm supplies, if they were in season, he always returned with peaches.

The Library that Gumbo Built

The Chamber of Commerce in the small fishing town of Carrabelle, on Florida's Forgotten Coast, holds an annual waterfront festival. In their 1997 gumbo cook-off, local home cook Jackie Gay's gumbo won first place.

Gay continued to perfect the recipe with a goal in mind. She submitted it to a *Good Housekeeping* magazine Recipe of the Year contest. The recipe won the Grand Prize, $50,000 from the Paul Newman Foundation. Gay designated the Franklin County Public Library system as her favorite charity. The community badly needed a new library.

The prize money along with other contributions created a new public library for Carrabelle; it was completed in 2002.

· · ·

Franklin County Florida's Own Frankly Fantastic Seafood Gumbo

Courtesy of the Carrabelle Library and Jackie Gay

2 Tbsp. vegetable oil

4 large onions, purple and yellow, sliced

4 bell peppers—red, green, and yellow, sliced

2 26-oz. jars Newman's Own Diavolo Sauce

3 cups water

1 Tbsp. Cajun seasoning

1 tsp. each of black and red pepper

1½ tsp. salt

1 pint fresh, shucked Apalachicola Bay oysters in liquid

2 lbs. fresh shrimp, peeled and deveined

1 lb. fresh scallops

1 lb. fresh cooked crab fingers (if available) or lump crabmeat

2 lbs. fresh grouper fillets (or other firm fish fillets like scrod) cut into 1-inch pieces

1 lb. fresh or frozen okra

12 cups hot cooked white rice (use very high-quality rice only)

Heat oil in an 8-quart Dutch oven or saucepot, over medium heat. Add onions and peppers and cook until slightly soft. Drain off excess oil.

Add Newman's Own Diavolo Sauce, water, and all seasonings, simmer for 30 minutes on low heat. Then, add all seafood and simmer for 45 minutes. Add okra and simmer for another 15 minutes. Serve immediately or refrigerate overnight and reheat slowly.

Spoon 1 cup gumbo over about 1/2 cup of hot rice. Saltine crackers on the side, if you'd like.

Serves 32.

• • •

Florida French Dressing

1 1/3 cup orange juice
1 cup salad oil
1/4 cup vinegar
1/2 tsp. Worcestershire sauce
1/2 tsp. paprika
1 small clove garlic, minced
2 Tbsp. lemon juice
1/3 cup confectioners' sugar
1/2 tsp. salt
1/4 tsp. mustard

Mix all together and shake in jar until blended. Makes 1 1/2 cups.

• • •

Southern Mashed Potato Salad

8 to 10 medium potatoes
1 1/2 tsp. salt
1/4 tsp. pepper
1/4 cup cider vinegar
1 1/4 cups mayonnaise
6 hard-cooked eggs, chopped
1 small jar pimientos, chopped
1/2 cup chopped green onion tops
1/4 cup chopped green pepper
1 cup chopped celery

Boil potatoes in salted water, covered, until tender. Drain well. In pot, mash until smooth. Stir in thoroughly salt, pepper, vinegar, and mayonnaise. Add eggs and all other ingredients; toss gently. Pack into ring mold, turn out, and serve while warm. May also be chilled and garnished with parsley or raw vegetables. Serves 10.

· · ·

Crisp Green Tomato Pickles

4 quarts thinly sliced green tomatoes
1 quart thinly sliced white onions
⅓ cup salt
3 cups white vinegar
1 tsp. whole allspice
2 tsp. whole black pepper
1 Tbsp. celery seed
2 Tbsp. white mustard seed
1 lemon, thinly sliced
2 drops red hot sauce
3 cups packed brown sugar

Sprinkle ⅓ cup salt on tomatoes and onion; leave overnight, covered. Drain. Place all remaining ingredients in pot; bring to boil and add tomatoes and onion. Bring to boil then reduce to simmer and cook about 10 minutes, stirring several times. Pour into hot sterilized jars and seal. Makes 5 pints.

· · ·

Honey Fruit Salad Dressing

1 cup heavy cream, whipped
3 Tbsp. honey
1 Tbsp. lime or lemon juice
⅛ tsp. ground mace

Beat cream just until stiff then beat in remaining ingredients. Use as dessert sauce over fresh or canned peaches, pineapple, pears, or other fruit.

···

Sunshine Chicken Salad

1½ cups cooked diced chicken
¼ cup diced celery
½ cup white grapes, halved
½ cup Creamy Fruit Dressing (below)
Salad greens
½ avocado, sliced
¼ cup chopped pecans
6 canned spiced crabapples

Add Creamy Fruit Dressing to chicken, celery, and grapes. Place greens on plates with salad in center. Sprinkle with chopped pecans; garnish with sliced avocado and crabapples. Serves 6.

Creamy Fruit Dressing:
2 tsp. salt
1 tsp. sugar
½ tsp. paprika
½ cup lemon juice
1½ cups salad oil
1⅓ cups heavy cream

In a jar, shake together all ingredients except cream. Gradually add the cream, beating with a rotary beater until thick. Makes 3⅓ cups; recipe may be halved, to make about 1¼ cups.

···

Roast Pork with Tropical, Five-Fruit Glaze

3-lb. boneless pork loin, trimmed of most fat and tied

For Glaze:
3 Tbsp. butter or margarine
3 Tbsp. apricot preserves
3 Tbsp. currant jelly
3 Tbsp. guava paste or jelly
1 Tbsp. lemon juice
2 Tbsp. Dijon mustard
2 Tbsp. orange liqueur (Triple Sec or Cointreau)

Spray roasting rack with vegetable oil and place in roasting pan lined with aluminum foil. Place roast in pan, fat side up; set aside. Make glaze by combining butter, preserves, jellies, lemon juice, and mustard in saucepan. Simmer until butter melts; add liqueur and cook 3 minutes more. Brush over pork roast.

Bake pork roast uncovered in 350°F oven 1½ to 2 hours, or until meat thermometer reads 170°F. During last 30 minutes of cooking time, baste several times with glaze mixture. Remove cooked roast from oven; let set 15 minutes before carving.

. . .

Mock Oysters

1 cup corn cut from cob (or frozen)
1 Tbsp. butter, melted
2 egg yolks, separated
½ tsp. salt
⅛ tsp. ground black pepper
Dash cayenne
¼ tsp. ground thyme
½ cup sifted all-purpose flour
Cooking oil
Celery salt

Combine corn, butter, egg yolks, seasoning, and flour. Beat egg whites until they stand in soft, stiff peaks and fold into mixture. Drop from teaspoon into deep cooking oil, preheated to 350°F. Fry until golden. Drain on paper towels. Sprinkle lightly with celery salt. Serve as appetizers. Makes 60.

. . .

Glorified Summer Squash

2 cups cooked yellow squash
¼ cup breadcrumbs
3 Tbsp. butter
½ cup milk
2 Tbsp. chopped onion
2 Tbsp. chopped green pepper
1 Tbsp. chopped pimiento

2 Tbsp. tomato ketchup
Salt, pepper to taste
¼ cup grated cheddar cheese
2 beaten eggs
1 cup buttered breadcrumbs
Paprika

Boil squash in salted water until tender. Mash fine; add all other
ingredients, except bread crumbs and paprika. Pour into buttered baking
dish. Top with buttered bread crumbs; sprinkle with paprika. Bake in
350°F oven until firm 25 to 30 minutes. Serves 4–6.

. . .

Old South Tomato Salad

3 medium tomatoes, sliced
1 onion cut into rings
Salad greens
⅓ cup French salad dressing
¼ tsp. celery seed
¼ cup pickle relish
6 slices crisp cooked bacon, crumbled
2 hard-cooked eggs, quartered
Monosodium glutamate

Arrange tomatoes and onion rings on crisp greens. Blend French dressing
with celery seed and pickle relish; pour over tomatoes and onions.
Sprinkle with monosodium glutamate; scatter bacon on top and garnish
with eggs.

Serves 6.

. . .

Southern Corn Pudding

3 eggs
2 cups cream-style canned corn
2 Tbsp. melted butter
2 cups scalded milk
2 tsp. salt
Dash pepper
2 Tbsp. flour

1 Tbsp. sugar cracker crumbs
Butter

Beat eggs well. Combine with all ingredients. Pour into buttered casserole. Sprinkle with crumbs; dot with butter. Place in pan of warm water. Bake in 325°F oven, uncovered, 1 hour 15 minutes. Serves 6.

. . .

Deviled Fresh Carrots

12 young tender carrots
1/2 cup butter or margarine
2 Tbsp. light brown sugar
1/4 tsp. salt
1 tsp. dry mustard
1/8 tsp. ground black pepper
Dash cayenne pepper

Wash carrots, peel, and cut each in half lengthwise. Sauté in butter 5 minutes. Add salt and spices. Cover and cook 10 minutes or until carrots are tender. Serve hot. Serves 6.

. . .

Buttermilk Biscuits

1 cup flour
2 tsp. baking powder
1/4 tsp. baking soda
1 tsp. salt
1 cup buttermilk
2 Tbsp. lard or ham fat

Measure 2 heaping tablespoons of flour and use to flour surface. Put remaining flour in bowl, make a hole in center of flour, and put into this the baking powder, baking soda, and salt. Add shortening; pour in buttermilk. With fingertips, gradually mix, using enough milk to make a soft dough. Turn onto floured surface and pat gently to 1/2-inch thickness. Cut out with biscuit cutter and place in greased pan. Bake at 400°F until brown on bottom (about 15 minutes) then place under broiler for a minute or two, if necessary to brown tops. Makes about 20 biscuits.

. . .

Pecan Waffles

2 cups sifted all-purpose flour
1 tsp. baking soda
1 Tbsp. sugar
1/2 tsp. salt
2 eggs, separated
1/4 cup vinegar
11/4 cups sweet milk
1/3 cup melted shortening
1/4 cup chopped pecans

Sift together flour, baking soda, sugar, and salt. Beat together egg yolks, vinegar, and milk, then mix with dry ingredients. Stir in melted shortening and pecans, stirring until smooth. Use mixer to beat egg whites until stiff but not dry; fold into batter. Pour on heated waffle iron; bake until steaming stops. Serve with warm syrup and butter. Serves 4.

. . .

Honey-Pecan Banana Bread

11/4 cups shortening
2 cups sugar
4 eggs
1 cup honey
21/2 cups mashed ripe bananas
5 cups sifted all-purpose flour
21/2 tsp. baking powder
21/2 tsp. baking soda

1 tsp. salt
2 cups chopped pecans

Cream shortening and sugar. Add eggs one at a time while creaming. Add honey and bananas; mix thoroughly. Sift flour, baking powder, soda, and salt together. Add to batter, mixing well. Fold in chopped pecans. Pour batter into three 4 × 8 × 2 1/2 inch loaf pans, lightly greased on bottom and sides, filling each slightly more than 1/4 full. Bake in 350°F oven 45 to 55 minutes or until tester comes out clean. Makes 3 loaves.

. . .

Honey Pecan Pie

Single 9-inch pie crust
3 eggs
1/3 cup granulated sugar
1/3 cup light brown sugar
1/4 tsp. salt
1/4 cup melted butter
1/2 cup honey
1/2 cup white corn syrup
1 tsp. vanilla
1 cup pecan halves

Beat eggs. Mix in all other ingredients except pecan halves; pour into pastry-lined 9-inch pie pan. Arrange pecan halves on filling in desired pattern. Bake 40 to 50 minutes at 375°F until set and pastry is golden. Cool. Serve cold or slightly warm.

. . .

Yam Praline Pie

2 eggs
1/2 cup granulated sugar
1/2 cup packed light brown sugar
1 tsp. cinnamon
1/2 tsp. nutmeg
1/2 tsp. ginger

Praline Topping:
1 1/3 cup chopped pecans

½ cup packed brown sugar
3 Tbsp. softened butter
2 cups cooked, mashed fresh yams
¼ cup milk
1 cup light cream
1 unbaked 9-inch pastry shell

Beat eggs in mixing bowl; beat in granulated and brown sugars, spices and salt. Blend in yams. Gradually stir in milk and cream. Pour into unbaked pastry shell. Bake in 400°F oven 10 minutes. Reduce heat to 350°F and bake 20 minutes. Combine topping ingredients; sprinkle over surface of pie. Continue baking 25 minutes until knife inserted near center comes out clean. Cool completely before serving.

English

In *The Atlanta Exposition Cookbook*, compiled by Mrs. Henry Lumpkin Wilson, for the Cotton States and International Exposition in 1895, countless recipes reveal their British origins. The trifle is among them. The first documented trifle recipe comes from 1585, and manifestations abound. Sponge cake (with or without alcohol), custard, preserves, fresh fruit, whipped cream, and almonds (a latecomer). Ingredients must be layered and visible through a glass bowl.

This light, festive dessert remains popular especially in the northern parts of the state, as a result of our neighbor, a former British colony, Georgia.

• • •

Strawberry Trifle

Courtesy of Jennifer Cerchiai

1 5-oz. package instant vanilla pudding mix
3 cups cold whole milk
1 9-inch angel food cake, cut into cubes
3 bananas, sliced

1 16-ounce package frozen strawberries, or use fresh
1 12-ounce container frozen whipped topping, thawed

Prepare pudding with milk according to package directions. In a trifle bowl or other glass serving dish, layer half the cake pieces, half the pudding, half the bananas, half the strawberries, and half the whipped topping. Repeat the layers. Cover and chill in the refrigerator 4 hours before serving.

Jennifer Cerchiai is Miami born and raised but recently moved to Atlanta, Georgia. This simple yet attractive trifle can be sprinkled with sliced almonds.

. . .

Creole Sweet Potato–Pecan Pie

9-inch unbaked pie shell
1/3 cup granulated white sugar
1/3 cup light brown sugar
1/4 tsp. salt
1/4 tsp. ground ginger
1/4 tsp. ground cinnamon
1/2 tsp. ground nutmeg
1/16 tsp. ground cloves
1 cup mashed sweet potatoes
2 well-beaten eggs
1/4 cup hot milk
1/2 cup light brown sugar
1/4 cup (1/2 stick) butter or margarine, softened
1/4 cup pecans, chopped medium-fine

Line 9-inch pie plate with unbaked pastry; set aside. Combine white and brown sugars, salt, and spices in mixing bowl. Blend in mashed sweet potatoes. Beat in eggs. Stir in hot milk. Pour into unbaked pie shell. Bake 25 minutes in preheated 375°F oven. Meanwhile, blend 1/2 cup brown sugar with butter or margarine and pecans. Sprinkle over partially baked pie. Continue baking 30 minutes or until filling is firm in center. Serve cold with whipped cream.

The Panhandle

Steep steps climb the crumbling brick wall of Fort San Carlos, built in Pensacola in 1787.

History was made in Pensacola, the second oldest city in the United States. In more than four centuries, the people have lived under 17 changes of government, and five flags: Spanish, French, British, Confederate, and American.

The first colony was founded when Tristan de Luna landed in Pensacola Bay with 1,500 persons in 1559, but a hurricane hit the fleet and the venture ended in just two years. Today, a cross in the sand marks the event.

After establishing St. Augustine in 1565, the Spanish returned to Pensacola in 1698 to build a fort. The French moved down the Mississippi and took the fort in 1719 but lost it again to the Spanish, and so it went.

After Great Britain ceded Florida to Spain in 1783, there were frequent Indian raids and Andrew Jackson waged successful attacks in Florida, then set up a military government in 1818. In 1821, he became provisional governor when Spain gave Florida up to the United States, and Pensacola was headquarters.

Important because it is the state's largest natural deep-water harbor, Pensacola had a U.S. Navy Yard built in 1825 and has remained an important military bastion since. Fort Pickens on Santa Rosa Island was a key Union stronghold during the War Between the States, when Union forces held the fort and imprisoned Geronimo Goyathlay, the legendary Apache warrior and medicine man, and 16 warriors. They arrived to the fort in 1886. By 1887, tourists began to visit the fort to see the famous prisoners.

Inside famous Pensacola Naval Air Station, where naval aviation was born, are Forts San Carlos, Barrancas, and Redoubt.

The Confederates were ordered to abandon the city in February 1862; supplies and troops were moved out. Most citizens left, burning what they could not carry, and by May, federal troops took over. There was a long listless period followed by the Reconstruction, then the timber and naval stores began moving out on new railroads.

The waterfront was improved during the busy 1870s, berthing ships from Italy and France, from England and Sweden. A disastrous fire swept the town in 1880, but by 1900, Pensacola was the second largest city in Florida with 18,000 residents. By 1910, population had grown to 22,982. Today it is about 357,000.

The U.S. government built its first training base for naval aviators there in 1914. This is one of the events recorded in the history of naval aviation from its beginnings to the space age, which is shown in the Naval Air Museum at the Naval Air Station.

This quiet city is thriving, but life continues at a pleasant, leisurely pace. Summers, this westernmost section of Florida is filled with Southern tourists flocking to the magnificent beaches of Santa Rosa Island, part of a great state park that offers swimming, fishing, and boating. The beaches are famous for their long stretches of pure white sand.

Hunting for quail, turkey, and deer is done in Apalachicola National Forest, which spreads over 600,000 acres and is the largest of the state's three national forests. And for fishing buffs, there is fun to be had angling for red snapper, tarpon, channel bass, sea trout, mackerel, amberjack, grouper, and more, from old Pensacola Bay Bridge—"the world's longest fishing pier." It is also known as the Three-Mile Bridge.

Pensacola itself is more Spanish than American and the wrought iron decorating the houses is a tipoff that, historically and architecturally, the town is more closely related to New Orleans and Mobile than to other Florida cities. Old balconies, graceful gables, and wrought-iron balustrades contribute to the romantic, Old World atmosphere along oak-shaded streets.

Pensacola has a proud group of "Creoles" with a African-Spanish heritage, as well as a prosperous African American population. Traditional cooking of the Old South blends with varied nationalities to create a unique cuisine.

It's an old Pensacola custom to have a "hospitality table" near the front door of each home at Christmas time, laden with fruit and homemade goodies.

Southern foods take on added Spanish and Creole spiciness in the steaming seafood chowders, crusty brown barbecued chicken and fish, Gaspachee (better known as Gazpacho) salad, homemade mincemeat, baked grits, Hoppin' John, and much more.

In magnolia-shaded Pensacola, and in other Florida towns and cities along the Gulf Coast—Fort Walton Beach, Panama City, Apalachicola— the unique handling of fresh seafood is superb, not to be missed!

Panhandle Specialties

...

Deviled Crabcakes

1 lb. crabmeat
1 cup cracker crumbs
3 eggs, lightly beaten
1/2 cup finely minced celery
1/2 cup minced green pepper
1 Tbsp. Worcestershire sauce
1/2 tsp. salt
1/2 tsp. black pepper
Few drops Tabasco
2 Tbsp. lemon juice
1 Tbsp. vinegar
1 cup melted butter
8 crab shells

Beat eggs lightly. Mix all ingredients lightly. Stuff into 8 crab shells. Bake at 375°F for about 12 minutes, until piping hot. Serves 8.

...

Pickled Shrimp

1 cup salad oil
1 cup white vinegar
Juice of 1/2 lemon
1 tsp. dill seed
1 tsp. peppercorns
1 stick cinnamon
1 tsp. whole cloves
1 tsp. salt
1 onion, sliced
2 lbs. cleaned, boiled shrimp

Cook together for 10 minutes first 8 ingredients. Cool. Slice onion and place in bowl with cold shrimp. Pour pickling mixture over shrimp; refrigerate overnight. (Keeps well up to a week.) Drain; serve as appetizer, or on a salad plate.

Oysters Pensacola

¼ cup grated onion
¼ cup finely chopped parsley
3 Tbsp. finely chopped celery
1 tsp. lemon juice
¼ tsp. salt
⅛ tsp. pepper
Few drops Tabasco
½ cup butter
3 dozen oysters on the half shell
Buttered crumbs

Cream butter then add onion, parsley, celery, lemon juice, and seasonings. Place oysters on half shell in shallow baking pan. Top each with a spoonful of the onion and butter mixture. Sprinkle with buttered crumbs and bake in 375°F oven about 30 minutes, until crumbs are brown. Serves 6.

The Patti Family

Joe Patti's Seafood has supplied Pensacola with seafood for 91 years. In 1919, its founder Joe Patti never got back on board his Italian ship that was docked in Brooklyn, New York. He moved to Pensacola where a small Italian community had settled and began working as a deck hand. He got a captain's license and bought a boat, married Anna in 1930, and began shrimping at night. Anna sold shrimp for bait off their porch. Along with great recipes and seafood handling tips, the story of the Patti family in Pensacola and the Panhandle and the evolution of an international business is told in their cookbook. Frank Patti Sr., at 91, still comes to the market to work, giving out numbers to customers as they wait their turn.

...

Blackened Redfish

1–1½ lbs. Redfish fillets
2 tsp. ground thyme
2 tsp. ground marjoram
2 tsp. garlic powder
1 tsp. ground oregano
1 tsp. cayenne
1 tsp. paprika
1 tsp. salt
1 tsp. white pepper
Margarine

Thaw fish if frozen. Mix all ingredients except margarine. Heat large, lightly oiled cast iron skillet over high heat until a drop of water sizzles in the pan, about 10 minutes. Coat both sides of the fish with margarine. Sprinkle fish with spices, shaking off excess. Place fillets in hot skillet and cook 2 to 3 minutes per side or until fish flakes easily when tested with a fork.

"Blackened Redfish" by the Patti family in *Joe Patti's Seafood and Favorite Family Recipes*. Birmingham: Seacoast Publishing Inc., 2012, p. 66. Reprinted with permission.

...

Emerald Coast Snapper

1 lb. snapper fillets
2 tsp. Dijon mustard
4 dried apricots, finely chopped
3 Tbsp. minced celery
2 Tbsp. toasted slivered almonds
¾ cup unsweetened orange juice
¼ tsp. white pepper
¾ cup chicken broth
1 tsp. Dijon mustard
½ tsp. white pepper
½ tsp. curry powder
2 tsp. cornstarch
1 Tbsp. dry sherry

Thaw fish if frozen. Spread inside of fillets with 2 teaspoons Dijon mustard. Combine apricots, celery, almonds, and ¼ teaspoon white pepper; mix well. Divide mixture on top of fillets. Roll fillets turban style and secure with a toothpick. Combine next five ingredients in a 10-inch frying pan; bring to a simmer. Lower fillets, seam side down, in simmering liquid; cover and simmer 5 to 6 minutes, turning fillets once after five minutes. Simmer 3 to 5 minutes longer. With a slotted spatula transfer fillets to a warm platter. Boil remaining liquid until mixture reduces to 1 cup. Combine cornstarch and sherry, mixing well; stir into poaching liquid. Boil, stirring constantly, 1 minute. Remove and discard toothpicks; spoon sauce over fillets. Serves 4.

"Emerald Coast Snapper" by the Patti family in *Joe Patti's Seafood and Favorite Family Recipes*. Birmingham: Seacoast Publishing Inc., 2012, p. 76. Reprinted with permission.

· · ·

Alligator Étouffée

1 lb. alligator meat, cut into thin strips
2 sticks butter
1/2 cup green onions, chopped
1/4 cup parsley, chopped
2 garlic cloves, minced
4 celery stalks, chopped
1 can tomatoes
Salt to taste
Cayenne and black pepper to taste

Sauté onions, garlic, and celery in butter until soft. Add tomatoes and simmer 20 minutes in covered iron pot. Add meat and cook over low heat until tender (about 1 hour). If gravy is too thick, add a small amount of hot water. Serve over rice.

"Alligator Etouffee" by the Patti family in *Joe Patti's Seafood and Favorite Family Recipes*. Birmingham: Seacoast Publishing Inc., 2012, p. 91. Reprinted with permission.

· · ·

Pasta and Oysters

1 medium to large onion, diced
1 large can tomato sauce
1/4 cup olive oil

2 sprigs fresh basil or 1 tsp. dried
1 tsp. sugar or artificial sweetener
2 pints oysters with juice
1 8-oz. package small-shell pasta
1 Tbsp. Romano cheese, grated
Salt and pepper to taste
Olive oil

Brown onion in olive oil. Add tomato sauce and ½ can of water. Cook
slowly for 15 minutes. Add basil and sugar. Let cook for 10 minutes
longer. Add oysters and juice; let cook for 10 to 15 minutes. Add enough
water for the amount of pasta; bring to a boil and add pasta. Cook until
pasta is done. Romano cheese is sprinkled over individual servings.

"Pasta & Oysters" by the Patti family in *Joe Patti's Seafood and Favorite
Family Recipes*. Birmingham: Seacoast Publishing Inc., 2012, p. 96.
Reprinted with permission.

. . .

Snapper Red and Green

1–1½ lb. red snapper fillets or steaks
2 tsp. lime juice
1 onion, chopped
1 green pepper, cut into 1¼-inch strips
2 cloves garlic, minced
2 Tbsp. olive oil
2 14-oz. cans whole, peeled tomatoes
⅛ tsp. ground red pepper (or to taste)
½ cup sliced green olives, pimiento-stuffed

Sprinkle snapper with lime juice and set aside at room temperature while
preparing sauce. In large skillet over medium-high heat, sauté onion,
green pepper, and garlic in oil until onion is tender. Add tomatoes and
liquid and red pepper. Cook 5 minutes, stirring occasionally. Arrange
fillets over sauce; scatter olives over fish. Reduce heat to low. Cook,
covered, until fish flakes with a fork (allow 10 minutes for each inch of
fillets, measured at thickest place). Serve snapper hot with sauce, adding
more olives if desired. Serves 2.

The Bushwacker

Born in 1975 at the Ship's Store, Sapphire Pub at Sapphire Village in St. Thomas, Virgin Islands, this creamy, chocolatey piña colada–like drink was a favorite with locals. Linda Taylor Murphy, the previous owner of the Sandshaker Lounge on Pensacola Beach, was visiting the islands. She loved the drink and brought it back to the Sandshaker, where she experimented with ingredients and found her own favorite way to make it.

The signature drink is popular on Pensacola Beach, throughout Florida, and beyond. Every August, the Sandshaker sponsors a Bushwacker Festival.

. . .

The Bushwacker Cocktail

1 oz. dark rum
1 oz. Kahlua
1 oz. Dark Crème de Cacao
2 oz. Cream of Coconut
2 oz. milk or half-and-half
1 cup ice

Put all the ingredients in a blender, then strain into a tall glass. Top with a cherry.

While some ingredients may be exchanged and many variations exist, this is a standard Bushwacker Cocktail recipe.

. . .

Baked Grits

1 cup milk
2 Tbsp. butter
2 cups cooked grits
2 eggs beaten until frothy

¹/₂ tsp. salt
Dash of pepper

Heat milk and butter. Add and mix until smooth the grits, eggs, salt, and pepper. Pour into buttered casserole and bake at 325°F until firm and golden brown, about 35 minutes. Serves 4–6.

• • •

Gaspachee

(Pensacola Salad)

2 hardtack or pilot bread
2 chopped cucumbers
2 chopped large ripe tomatoes
1 chopped green pepper
1 medium onion, chopped
4 chopped stalks of celery
About ¹/₄ cup mayonnaise
Salt, pepper to taste

Soak hardtack in water for about ten minutes. Squeeze dry of all water; add vegetable ingredients, mayonnaise, salt, and pepper. (Be sure the vegetables are very finely chopped and well chilled, for best flavor.)

The hardtack made today is not as rock hard as that of early times, so it needs only a brief soaking. (If hardtack is not available in your area, you can order it from Premier Bakery, 1124 West Garden Street, Pensacola, 32501.)

• • •

Southern Spoon Bread

4 cups milk
1 cup white cornmeal
2 Tbsp. butter
1¹/₂ tsp. salt
1 tsp. double-acting baking powder
4 well-beaten eggs

Every Florida pioneer has a favorite recipe!

Over hot water in double boiler, scald milk; gradually add cornmeal and continue to cook and stir until thick. Add butter, salt, and baking powder; mix well. Then add hot mixture slowly to beaten eggs, stirring constantly. Pour into greased 2-quart casserole. Bake in 425°F oven 45 minutes or until set. Serve at once in baking dish with plenty of butter. Serves 8.

. . .

Shrimp Creole

1/2 lb. salt pork
2 medium onions, chopped
1 10 1/4 -oz. can tomato soup
1 4-oz. can tomato paste
1 medium green pepper, chopped
2 celery stalks, chopped
2 15-oz. cans tomatoes
Salt, pepper, Worcestershire to taste
3 lbs. shrimp
2 cups uncooked rice

Dice salt pork and fry until crisp and brown in heavy skillet. Remove bacon from pan, leaving all melted drippings in skillet. Add chopped onions, pepper, and celery to pan drippings; simmer until soft. Add tomatoes, soup, and tomato paste. Season to taste with salt, pepper, and Worcestershire. Cook on low heat until thick, about 2 hours, stirring occasionally.

While sauce is cooking, prepare shrimp. Rinse well under cool, running water. Cook in large pot containing 3 or more quarts of boiling, salted water 10 to 12 minutes, just until shells turn pink. Remove from heat, cool in cooking water about 20 minutes, drain. When cool, remove shells and devein.

Add shrimp to cooked sauce, saving 6–8 large shrimp to garnish top. Cook rice according to package directions, cover with Shrimp Creole, and garnish. Serves 8.

···

Hoppin' John

2 cups black-eyed peas
1/4 lb. lean salt pork, sliced
2 cups cooked rice
Salt and pepper to taste
Dash of Tabasco

Wash peas and soak overnight. Drain. Add sliced salt pork. Cover with salted water and cook about 40 minutes, or until tender. Some liquid should remain in the pan; if not, add enough to cover bottom of pan. Stir in cooked rice and seasonings. Place over low heat and stir; cover and heat. Serve immediately. Serves 4–6.

Peanutty Recipes

···

Baked Apples with Peanut Topping

4 medium apples
1/3 cup raisins
1/2 cup orange juice
1/2 cup water
2 Tbsp. flour
1/8 tsp. salt
1/4 cup sugar
1/2 tsp. cinnamon
1 tsp. grated orange rind
1 1/2 Tbsp. butter
1 1/2 Tbsp. peanut butter
1/4 cup chopped salted peanuts

Core apples without cutting through the blossom end. Pare apples one-third of way down. Put raisins into centers of apples. Place apples in a baking dish and pour orange juice and water around them. Combine flour, salt, sugar, cinnamon, orange rind, butter, and peanut butter, mixing until crumbly. Stir in peanuts. Spoon mixture over apples, piling some in a mound on top. Bake at 375°F about 1 hour, basting with the liquid every 15 minutes. The top of the filling may be toasted by placing in the broiler the last 5 minutes. Serves 4.

. . .

Peanut Butter Sauce for Vegetables

1 Tbsp. butter or margarine
1/4 cup peanut butter
2 tsp. flour
1/2 tsp. salt
Pepper
1 cup milk

Melt butter in pan over boiling water. Blend in the peanut butter. Add flour and seasonings and stir until smooth. Stir in milk slowly. Cook over boiling water until thick, stirring constantly. Serve on cooked cabbage, onions, or cauliflower. Makes about 1 cup.

. . .

Creamed Celery with Peanuts

1 1/2 cups celery cut in 1-inch pieces
1/4 cup liquid (cooking liquid plus milk)
1 Tbsp. flour
1/4 tsp. salt
Pepper
1 Tbsp. butter or margarine
1/4 cup grated cheese
1/4 cup chopped salted peanuts

Cook celery until tender in small amount of boiling salted water. Drain, retaining liquid. Measure cooking liquid and add enough milk to make 1/4 cup. Mix flour and part of liquid until smooth. Stir into rest of liquid. Add seasonings and butter; cook slowly until sauce thickens, stirring frequently. Stir celery and cheese into the sauce. As soon as cheese melts, remove from heat. Add peanuts. Serves 4.

Peanut Butter Muffins

1 cup sifted flour
2 tsp. baking powder
1 tsp. salt
1/4 cup sugar
1 1/3 cups peanut butter
2 eggs, beaten
1 cup milk
2 Tbsp. melted butter or margarine

Sift dry ingredients together. Work in peanut butter. Combine eggs and milk; pour into dry ingredients. Add butter and stir just enough to moisten dry ingredients. Fill greased muffin pans 2/3 full and bake in 400°F oven 25 minutes. Makes 12 large muffins.

Boiled Peanuts in the Slow Cooker

Courtesy of Tim Robb

1–2 lbs. raw/green peanuts
1/4–1/3 cup salt
Water

Wash peanuts in sink. Now they can either soak overnight in water or be put in the slow cooker. An overnight soak saturates the shells and keeps them from floating (as much) at the top of the slow cooker when cooking starts. It reduces cooking time.

Fill your slow cooker with water about a quarter of the way and add salt. Stir until combined, then fill with peanuts. Add more water until the peanuts are at the top of the slow cooker but can still be covered with the lid. The average slow cooker will hold about 1 1/2 to 2 pounds of peanuts. Stir until all peanuts are wet. Place lid on slow cooker. Cook on high

Tim Robb first tasted boiled peanuts when he traveled with his church youth group to Central Florida for a day of tubing on the Ichetucknee River. A friend invited him to try some, and Robb has been a fan of boiled peanuts since. Years later, he learned to make them on the stove top, then switched to a slow cooker.

Raw green peanuts prevail during the summer months and are found typically at farmers markets, produce stands, or grocery stores.

roughly 6–12 hours. If soaked, cook for 6 hours then taste for firmness and saltiness. If not soaked, continue to cook for hours until desired texture is achieved. Some people prefer a firmer texture; others like them mushy.

If you prefer them softer and saltier, add more salt (about a half cup total) and cook longer. Taste every two hours to see if they meet your preferences. Once boiled, they will last 3–4 days in the refrigerator or frozen for 2–4 months.

Flavor variations:

These added ingredients must be added at the beginning of the cooking cycle so they will be absorbed into the peanuts.

Florida-Style Hot and Spicy Peanuts: add 6–10 minced Datil peppers.

Garlic Peanuts: add 3–6 tablespoons garlic powder or garlic cloves, about 6–10 fresh cloves or 2–3 tablespoons of minced garlic from a jar.

Other spicy variations include adding Creole seasoning or hot pepper sauce like Franks, Texas Pete, or Louisiana Hot Sauce, or other types of hot peppers like jalapeños or Ghost peppers, depending on taste.

George Washington Carver

Agricultural scientist, inventor, educator, and humanitarian, George Washington Carver created more than 300 food, industrial, and commercial products from peanuts. He revolutionized agriculture by inventing crop rotation to improve depleted soils. He was the first African American to receive a bachelor's degree in science in 1894. Franklin D. Roosevelt signed legislation for the George Washington Carver National Monument in Diamond, Missouri, an honor previously reserved only for presidents.

RECIPE INDEX